People weekly

March 1, 1974    35 Cents

**Mia Farrow**
In 'Gatsby,'
the year's next
big movie

PLUS **Inside Tom Cruise & Penélope's Breakup**

People

Special Double Issue

**30th Anniversary!**

SCANDALS
ROMANCES
FASHION
FIASCOES
UNSOLVED
MYSTERIES
& MORE

**MY BIGGEST MOMENT**
BY Julia Roberts
Mel Gibson
Muhammad Ali
Madonna
Cher
Faith Hill

JESSICA SIMPSON
Funny Girl, 2004

APRIL 12, 2004

# 30 YEARS OF SEEING STARS

# CONTENTS

SIREN OF THE '70s
A charter Charlie's Angel, Farrah Fawcett was a pinup en route to a roller-coaster career.

**THE '80s GODDESS**
Diana Spencer, our princess charming, adorned the PEOPLE cover more than 50 times.

**THE NOW PAIR**
In 2000, Brad Pitt became PEOPLE's only two-time Sexiest Man and Jennifer Aniston's friend for life.

# 1995-2004

## 92

### Icons

Talk shows were growing stale until **David Letterman, Oprah Winfrey** and **Ellen DeGeneres** injected new juice into the old genre. **Beyoncé** and **Britney** did some moving and shaking on the pop scene. And two favorite sons, **Prince William** and **JFK Jr.,** came into their own, but one left us too soon

### 120 Real World

Whether they were living in a mansion for *The Bachelorette,* on a tropical island for *Survivor* or in a penthouse suite for *The Apprentice,* contestants bared their souls—and then some—as they vied for the dream date/dream prize/dream job

### 122 First-Name Basis

Their distinctive tags—or work—made their surnames superfluous. **Angelina, Leo, Gwyneth** or **Charlize** said it all in Hollywood. **Eminem, P. Diddy** and **Christina**? Music's edgiest artists. **Matt & Katie** branded the right blend of charm and chemistry to be our breakfast partners of choice. And if it's **Paris,** well, it's complicated....

### 132 Falls from Grace

**Janet Jackson** upstaged a Super Bowl with a "wardrobe malfunction." Minnelli and Gest ringmastered a sad circus. **Rosie, Winona** and **Martha** found themselves headlining on Court TV. And the **Monica Lewinsky-Bill Clinton** scandal nearly ended a presidency

### 138 Fads & Fashions

**Botox** shots were the new wrinkle (remover), **Starbucks** coffeehouses were on every corner, and the **TiVo** recorder seemed like a keeper. But attention, **trucker hats, pashmina shawls** and **scooters:** Your 15 minutes are up!

Editor **ELIZABETH SPORKIN** Senior Editor **RICHARD BURGHEIM** Art Director **BESS WONG** Photo Editors **BRIAN BELOVITCH, JEN LOMBARDO** Writers **VICTORIA BOUGHTON, ELIZABETH O'BRIEN MOORE, JOANNA POWELL, LISA RUSSELL, ERICKA SOUTER, JENNIFER WULFF** Chief of Reporters **RANDY VEST** Researchers **SONA CHARAIPOTRA, LAURA DOWNEY, TOBY KAHN** Production Artist **LISA BURNETT** Scanner **RASHIDA MORGAN** Copy Editor **JENNIFER BROUGHEL** Special thanks to: Jane Bealer, Nick Brennan, Robert Britton, Luciana Chang, Sal Covarrubias, Urbano DelValle, Ian Devaney, Will Eisenberg, Maura Foley, Brien Foy, Margery Frohlinger, Patricia Hustoo, Spencer Kimmins, Maddy Miller, Charles Nelson, Susan Radlauer, Annette Rusin, Jack Styczynski, Gloria Truc, Céline Wojtala, Patrick Yang

**TIME INC. HOME ENTERTAINMENT**
President **ROB GURSHA** Vice President, Branded Businesses **DAVID ARFINE** Vice President, New Product Development **RICHARD FRAIMAN** Executive Director, Marketing Services **CAROL PITTARD** Director, Retail & Special Sales **TOM MIFSUD** Director of Finance **TRICIA GRIFFIN** Assistant Marketing Director **NIKI WHELAN** Prepress Manager **EMILY RABIN** Associate Book Production Manager **SUZANNE JANSO** Associate Product Manager **TAYLOR GREENE**

Special thanks to: Bozena Bannett, Alexandra Bliss, Bernadette Corbie, Robert Dente, Gina Di Meglio, Anne-Michelle Gallero, Peter Harper, Robert Marasco, Natalie McCrea, Jonathan Polsky, Margarita Quiogue, Mary Jane Rigoroso, Steven Sandonato, Grace Sullivan

## Jackie Onassis

By 1975 Jacqueline Bouvier Kennedy Onassis was living on her own in a gracious 15-room Manhattan apartment. (Her estranged second husband, Greek shipping magnate Aristotle Onassis, died that March.) Camelot had ended a decade before, but Jackie, wrote PEOPLE, was still "unofficial First Lady of the World." She had traded her JFK-era pillbox hats and pearls for dark glasses, head scarves and classic trench coats. She was understated, chic and thoroughly modern—not least in her decision, despite a $200 million fortune, to take a job at Doubleday, editing a dozen books a year. As a cultural activist, Jackie wielded her clout to preserve New York landmarks. Privately she saw Maurice Tempelsman, a Belgian-born financier and diamond merchant. Ultimately, though, motherhood mattered most. Shepherding Caroline and John Kennedy Jr. into adulthood was, she confided, "the best thing I have ever done." In 1994, by then a grandma of three, Jackie began treatment for non-Hodgkin's lymphoma. Within three months, John Jr. announced that his mother, 64, had died "surrounded by her friends and her family and her books. She did it her own way and in her own terms." It was a mercy, perhaps, that she did not live to see the tragic death of John Jr. himself.

## 1974-1984

# ICONS

From the most stylish (Jackie) to The Greatest (Ali) to the wildest (Cher), they were the headliners of PEOPLE's premiere decade

# Farrah Fawcett

Hers was the grin and body that launched 8 million posters, the coif copied by countless fans. For one giddy, jiggly season on *Charlie's Angels,* 1976-77, Farrah Fawcett-Majors was World Sex Symbol No. 1. Still, she insisted, "there's more to me than just hair and a smile." But first there had to be less. Her *Angels* contract had stipulated her being home to cook dinner for *Six Million Dollar Man* hubby Lee Majors. In 1979 she dropped him and the hyphenated name and began to impress critics in demanding roles in the TV film *The Burning Bed,* Off-Broadway and onscreen in *Extremities* and, in '97, in Robert Duvall's *The Apostle.* Though more recently indulging her inner flake on *Letterman* and in a nude video, she explained, "I don't want to spend my whole life being predictable."

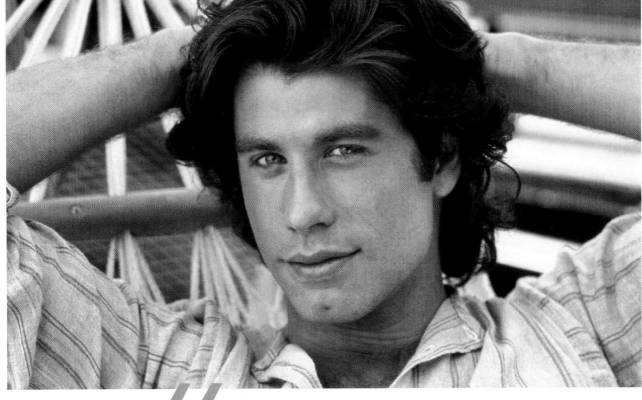

# John Travolta

**I always said one film makes you and one film remakes you. And I've had approximately six comebacks"**

He found fame in 1975 as *Welcome Back, Kotter*'s sweet, dim-witted Sweathog Vinnie Barbarino, and within two years John Travolta had an Oscar nomination and had helped prolong discomania in *Saturday Night Fever.* But after 1980's *Urban Cowboy,* he went into box office eclipse, and perhaps his most memorable moment of the next decade was whirling in the White House with Di. Then in '94 he rebounded with another Oscar nod as a junkie hit man in *Pulp Fiction.* The rest of his life was high-flying with wife Kelly Preston, two kids and a personal air fleet. "People related to him in every part," said *Phenomenon* costar Kyra Sedgwick. "He makes you see humanity in all the different roles."

# Dolly Parton

A buxom "Backwoods Barbie" in skintight getups and mile-high hair, Dolly Parton is an endearing mix of sass, rhinestoned flash and songwriting genius. A protégée of country legend Porter Wagoner, she hymned her impoverished East Tennessee youth (she was the fourth of 12 children) in her plaintive signature tune, "Coat of Many Colors." Then, in duets like "Islands in the Stream" with Kenny Rogers, she showed off a pop sensibility as sharp as her five-inch stilettos. After enjoying a brief film career, including *9 to 5* (for which she wrote an Oscar-nominated theme song) and *Steel Magnolias,* Parton built a flourishing Tennessee theme park called Dollywood. Details of her 38-year marriage to elusive asphalt paving contractor Carl Dean were scant, but on almost every other subject—her plastic surgeries, her myriad diets, a mid-'80s battle with depression—Parton has been ever candid. "I'll always be too much for some people," Parton summed it up, "but I'll never be enough for me."

# Robert De Niro

It was a simple question—"You talkin' to me?"—but *Taxi Driver's* Travis Bickle was the stuff of nightmares. The actor who played him, Robert De Niro, "is a strange, dark figure," said his *Godfather: Part II* director Francis Ford Coppola. "But he has the talent and the conceptual ability, and he works hard." Obsessively hard, including putting on 50-plus lbs. for *Raging Bull* and moonlighting in a cab before *Taxi Driver*. While the two-time Oscar winner (for *Bull* and *Godfather II*) has lately flexed his comic muscle with *Analyze This* and *Meet the Parents,* he won't shy from his sinister signature roles. "I don't mind being a bastard," said the twice-divorced father of five, "just as long as I am an interesting bastard."

# Meryl Streep

Just four years after leaving the rarefied air of the Yale Drama School, Meryl Streep was conquering Hollywood with quietly compelling performances in *The Deer Hunter* and *Kramer vs. Kramer.* "If there's a heaven for directors, it would be to direct Meryl Streep your whole life," said the late Alan J. Pakula. It was in his *Sophie's Choice* that she learned Polish to play the Holocaust survivor and perhaps best displayed her dogged work ethic. Her mastery of a globe's worth of accents—French, Australian, even Okie—and her chameleon-like immersion in roles have won her a permanent spot on the A list. "There's nothing she can't do," said *Kramer* director Robert Benton. Her 13 Oscar nominations, two trophies (for *Sophie's Choice* and *Kramer*) and four children are proof of that. "My wish for the world," said Pakula, "is that Meryl will someday be 90 years old, acting in a great role written about a 90-year-old woman."

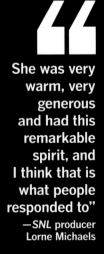

> **She was very warm, very generous and had this remarkable spirit, and I think that is what people responded to"**
> —*SNL* producer Lorne Michaels

# Gilda Radner

She must have been ready for prime time. The alum of Toronto's Second City troupe was the first member signed to *Saturday Night Live*'s founding 1975 cast. Gilda Radner was willing to play gawky, unglamorous roles like teenage nerd Lisa Loopner—and the public loved her for it. Even when in character as the obnoxious Roseanne Roseannadanna, "there's something very gentle and sweet in Gilda that comes through," wrote critic Molly Haskell. After creating another memorable broadcaster, Baba Wawa, Radner left *SNL* and in 1984 wed Gene Wilder. She used Roseannadanna's catchphrase—"it's always something"—for the title of a 1989 book detailing her battle with ovarian cancer. It was a fight she lost later that year at 42.

# Sylvester Stallone

It was a scenario even Hollywood couldn't have concocted. A self-described street tough turned actor wrote a screenplay about a dead-end club fighter who lands a heavyweight title bout and finds love. Shot for $1 million, *Rocky* got 10 Oscar nods (winning three, including Best Picture of 1976), grossed nearly $120 million and had critics hailing its star, Sylvester Stallone, as the next Brando. "Boy, that's a picture I wish I had made," said the late director Frank Capra, the king of the little-guy-bucking-the-system genre. Stallone wound up more of a brand than Brando, headlining four *Rocky* sequels. In '82 he took on another iconic role, vigilante Vietnam vet John Rambo in *First Blood,* launching a new tough-guy trilogy. Married three times, with five children, Stallone also ventured outside the action-hero arena, earning kudos (*Cop Land*) and hoots (*Rhinestone*). "I want people to say, 'He gave everything he had to it,'" he observed. "'He didn't just rest on his laurels.' I don't want anyone to say of me, 'His fire went out and he didn't know how to reignite it.'"

> The Bible is action-packed. The Koran is action-packed. Even Buddha had a few moments of suspense in his life"
> —On action films' bad rap

# Cher

"Unless you risk looking foolish," Cher once said, "you never have the possibility of being great." Between her outrageously revealing Bob Mackie gowns, her roller-coaster love life and her brazen chitchat ("The trouble with some women is they get all excited about nothing—and then they marry him"), shock and awe were her MO. She clamorously split from her supposed Svengali, Sonny Bono, in 1975, then filed for divorce nine days after marrying Gregg Allman (but stuck with him for two years). She did diligently cut almost an album per year to support kids Chastity and Elijah Blue (one by each husband). But she caused titters with her plastic-surgery confessions and her penchant for mostly younger men like Val Kilmer (13 years her junior) and "Bagel Boy" Rob Camilletti (18 years younger). Eyebrows really rose when she was cast opposite Meryl Streep in *Silkwood,* but she met the challenge with an Oscar-nominated performance and then took a trophy home for the romantic charmer *Moonstruck.* Meanwhile, she continued releasing hits like "Believe" into the '90s, and could her '02 Farewell Tour have really meant calling it quits? "There's a saying among those who work around Cher," noted a pop critic. "If there's a nuclear war, only two species will survive: the cockroaches and Cher."

# Muhammad Ali

He was as proficient with his tongue as he was with his fists, and is the first to tell you. "I am the onlyest of boxing's poet laureates," he once declared. After winning an Olympic gold medal and dethroning heavyweight champ Sonny Liston, he changed his "slave name" of Cassius Clay Jr. to the Islamic Muhammad Ali. A man of principle, he was stripped of his title and had his boxing license revoked for two and a half years as a conscientious objector to the Vietnam War. "The Greatest"—as he dubbed and proved himself—put the sweetness in the sweet science, imbuing his prowess in the ring with a sly playfulness. His verbal sparring with famed sportscaster Howard Cosell—"Man, without me you'd just be a mouth and a microphone"—was equal parts theater and genuine friendship. Ali won 56 of his 61 bouts, including the "Rumble in the Jungle" against George Foreman and the "Thrilla in Manila" against Joe Frazier in the mid-'70s. But the years of punishment may have led to the onset of Parkinson's disease in the early '80s. He no longer stings like a bee, but he still floats with a butterfly's grace as a joyful, globe-traveling humanitarian. "I want my health back," the four-times-wed dad of nine once said. "But I ain't sufferin'."

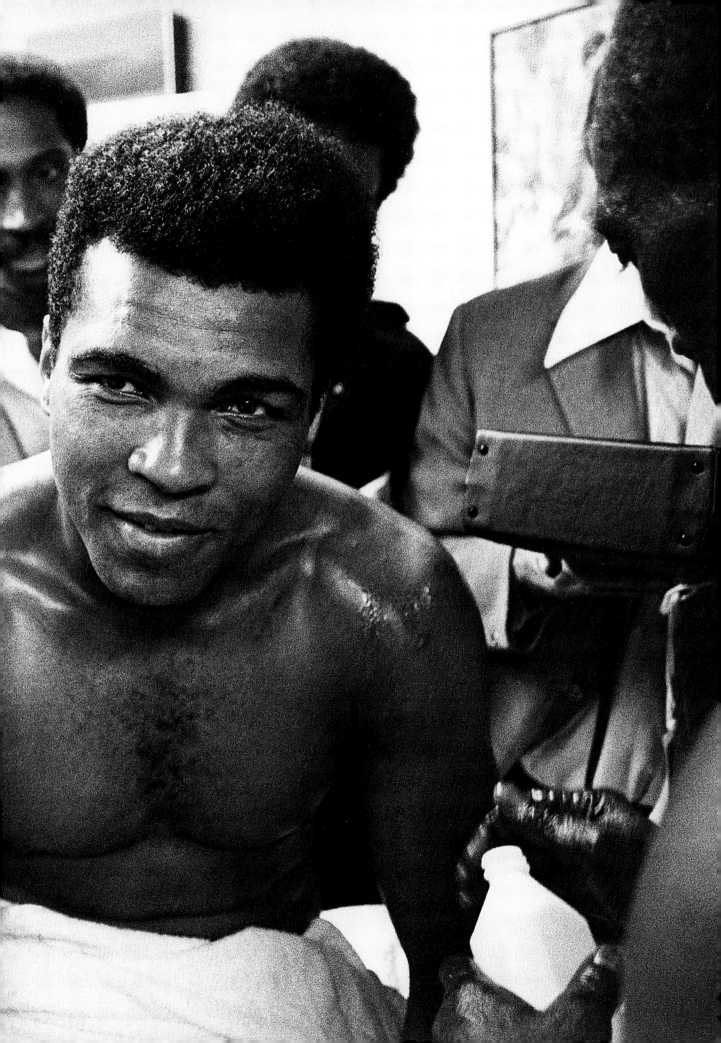

# Barbra Streisand

She has come a very long way from Brooklyn, with super determination and a voice that, on a clear day, can be heard in heaven (and on 40-plus gold albums). Broadway's original *Funny Girl* (and an Oscar winner for the film adaptation) became La Streisand and "Babs" to legions of fans, who adore her for, among other things, refusing to alter her nose. She proudly played up her Jewish heritage opposite Waspy Robert Redford in the hit weeper *The Way We Were* and a decade later in *Yentl,* which she produced, directed and starred in as a girl masquerading as a male yeshiva student. She was also a triple-tasker in the psychological saga *The Prince of Tides.* "Barbra never says, 'That's good enough,'" noted musical collaborator Marilyn Bergman of her legendary perfectionism. Married since '98 to actor James Brolin (she has a son with first husband Elliott Gould), Streisand offers no apologies for her controlling style and outspoken liberal politics. "When I hear my own overture play, I say, 'My God! You mean I sang all those songs?'" she said. "Now it's kind of a wonderful thing, to appreciate my own career."

# Robert Redford

It would have been easy to coast on his golden-boy charm, but Robert Redford chose instead to evolve into a director and environmental activist with ideals as glowing as his looks. He had proved he could play well with others, including Paul Newman in *Butch Cassidy and the Sundance Kid,* Barbra Streisand in *The Way We Were* and Dustin Hoffman in the Watergate chronicle *All the President's Men.* Then in 1981 he won an Oscar for his directorial debut in *Ordinary People.* Yet the proudest credit for the divorced father of three was the 1981 founding of the Sundance Institute to support small, independent films. "I simply wanted to get the movies seen," said Redford. "Plus, I admit, there was some perversity there. I loved the idea of dragging all these Hollywood folks into the Utah mountains in the winter."

# Goldie Hawn

"Being called a ditzy blonde doesn't bother me," Goldie Hawn once said. It didn't seem to bother audiences either, who embraced the onetime *Rowan & Martin's Laugh-In* regular and Oscar winner (for *Cactus Flower*). "The public responds to Goldie," said *First Wives Club* costar Diane Keaton. "She has a lovability that's rare, rare, rare, rare." After starring in such era-defining films as *Shampoo* and *Butterflies Are Free*, Hawn proved there was a method to her blondness. Paving the way for a new crop of female film execs, she produced (and starred in) 1980's *Private Benjamin* so she could call her own shots. "I'm a very practical person," she said. "As I got older, I stayed realistic." Twice divorced, she stayed grounded too, raising four children with longtime partner Kurt Russell—and becoming recently, gulp, a grandmother (to daughter Kate Hudson's son Ryder). Said Russell: "I'm enchanted by Goldie." Aren't we all?

You only lie to two
people in your
life: your girlfriend
and the police.
Everybody else you
tell the truth to"

# Jack
## Nicholson

If he didn't exist, Hollywood would have had to invent him: a sly guy with eloquent eyebrows and what TIME called a "shark's grin." Jack Nicholson turned it all into more Oscar nods (12) than any other gent, playing a rogues' gallery of rakes, rebels, roués and reprobates with steely precision and hammy flair. He varoomed into *Easy Rider* in 1969 and has made portraying angst and mania look easy ever since. "He's arguably the best actor of most people's lifetime," said James L. Brooks, who directed Nicholson to two of his three Oscars, in *As Good as It Gets* and *Terms of Endearment*. "He continues not to make any safe choices." Onscreen—or off. The avowed hedonist ("How I do love to play!") has squired a string of lovelies and fathered four children with three women. He's "much sweeter than people think he is," said Cher of her costar in *The Witches of Eastwick*. "Being in Jack's presence is like being in the grip of a great novel," added Harvey Keitel. "There's hundreds of people inside him, a whole world."

## The Reagans

Long before they were the President and First Lady, they were a couple hopelessly in love, he calling her "Mommy," she watching out for her "Ronnie." When Ronald and Nancy Reagan hit Washington in 1981, they continued the romance that had begun 32 years earlier in Hollywood, when he was an actor (*Knute Rockne—All American*) and future governor of California and she a rising starlet who decided that "being his wife was the role I wanted to play." She displayed a flair for glamorous gowns and entertaining—the likes of Frank Sinatra came and danced at state dinners. A onetime *G.E. Theater* TV host, Reagan was called the Great Communicator for his ability to disarm even critics of his conservative politics with a homespun, Illinois-bred forthrightness. He bounced back from a 1981 assassination attempt as ebullient as ever. Their strong bond withstood strains with their two children, Patti and Ron Jr. (He had two kids from his earlier marriage to actress Jane Wyman.) But their closeness was never more evident than in 1994, when Reagan, then 83, announced that he had Alzheimer's disease. His wife embarked on the increasingly lonely vigil of tending to the former leader, by now confined to their Bel Air home and unable to recognize even old friends. "Nancy's whole life has been Ronnie," said one of them, producer A.C. Lyles. "Her love for him is eternal."

# Al
## Pacino

A street-smart Shakespearean schooled on Off-Broadway stages, Al Pacino created some of film's most memorable roles playing a succession of hoods, creeps, losers and the rare hero. He owned the '70s with Oscar nods for the first two *Godfather* movies, *Serpico* and *Dog Day Afternoon.* His devout Method-actor intensity was legendary. "If the day's work demanded a lunatic, he was a lunatic all day long," recalled *Dog Day* director Sidney Lumet. Offscreen, however, "he's sort of the opposite of his characters," said longtime actor-coach friend Charlie Laughton. "He's very gentle and compassionate." Linked with former leading ladies like Diane Keaton and Marthe Keller, he never married but is father to three children, including twins with actress Beverly D'Angelo. Copping an Oscar—after eight nominations—for 1992's *Scent of a Woman* took Pacino by surprise. "It wasn't for a few days or even weeks that I started to feel the impact and the joy of it," he said. "You feel what it must feel like to be a winner."

# Bruce
## Springsteen

What Dylan was to the '60s, Bruce Springsteen was to the next generation. He was the blue-collar Boss of rock, a poet giving voice to teen yearnings and working-class woes. His anthems of everyday dreams and fears, loves and losses, won 10 Grammys plus an Oscar for "Streets of Philadelphia." Albums like *Born to Run* and *Darkness on the Edge of Town* went multiplatinum. "He's the most giving, energetic performer there ever was," said *New York Times* critic Stephen Holden of Springsteen's four-hour marathon concerts with the E Street Band. "No other performer has ever developed the kind of relationship Bruce has with his audience." His "Born in the U.S.A.," the bitter saga of a returning Vietnam vet, connected with an unlikely fan: President Reagan, whose use of the song in his reelection bid Springsteen protested. True to his roots, the Boss still lives in New Jersey with second wife Patti Scialfa and their three children. "I see myself more like a good journeyman," he once said of his career. "You do your job, you pass on some part of the flame . . . and you stir things up a little bit if you can."

# Sally Field

A nun who could fly had nothing on an actress who could transcend such a role and go on to become one of the formidable talents of her generation. While her transition from TV's *The Flying Nun* and *Gidget* to film was less than auspicious—in the lowbrow but crowd-pleasing *Smokey and the Bandit*—Sally Field wasted no time making up for it. Gritty roles in *Norma Rae* and *Places in the Heart* won her two Oscars and the admiration of her peers. "In all honesty, the one [actor] I want to emulate every time I go before the camera is Sally Field," said Tom Hanks, her costar in both *Forrest Gump* and *Punchline*. "I think she's a genius." Known for her wholesome image, she once said, "I'm just as sick of my 'good people' as audiences must be. I'd love to play a bitch or some women you don't really end up liking a whole lot." She maintained her Serious Actress status (sans bitches) in such films as *Absence of Malice,* but the twice-divorced mother of three made no apologies for more frothy fare like the *Smokey* sequel (with onetime beau Burt Reynolds). And her infamous Oscar acceptance speech? "I think I can get up there and say, 'You like me, you like me!' as many times as I want," she later said. "I've earned that right."

# Burt Reynolds

Building on the success of *The Longest Yard* (1974) and the *Smokey and the Bandit* franchise and right through *The Cannonball Run* in the early '80s, Burt Reynolds was simply the biggest male star in Hollywood. His macho breakthrough performance in *Deliverance* (1972) had made him famous—just as his undraped appearance in *Cosmopolitan* magazine the same year had made him notorious. Between marriages (*Laugh-In*'s Judy Carne for a couple of years in the '60s; *WKRP*'s Loni Anderson for six years ending in '94), Reynolds, a former Florida State football star and the son of a small-town police chief, conducted well-publicized romances with Dinah Shore, Sally Field and Chris Evert. And after his box office peak he kept working, collecting an Emmy in 1991, as a high school coach in CBS's *Evening Shade,* and his first Oscar nomination as a porn king in 1997's *Boogie Nights.* His OPEC-level testosterone production offset by a self-deprecating good ol' boy charm, he was, said *Boogie Nights* director Paul Thomas Anderson, "the coolest guy on the planet."

# Jane Fonda

In 1982 Americans, out-of-shape and uninterested in doing anything about it, first heard Jane Fonda intone the words: "Are you ready to do the workout?" What followed was an unprecedented marketing blitz: 17 million Jane Fonda workout tapes sold, making it the No. 1 nondramatic video in history. Years before reinvention was even in the lexicon, Fonda had pulled off another remarkable one. The daughter of Henry Fonda, she had steamed up the screen—under the direction of French first husband Roger Vadim—in *Barbarella* in 1968. Next, as the '70s dawned, she split from Vadim, morphed into an antiwar activist and wed Chicago Seven defendant Tom Hayden. She was later married for a decade to media mogul Ted Turner and became a born-again Christian. Through it all she developed into an actress of intensity and grace with Oscar-winning performances in *Klute* (1971) and *Coming Home* (1978). In 1981, at age 43, she fulfilled a life-long dream, costarring with her father in *On Golden Pond,* his last movie.

# Brooke Shields

She's never not been famous—or gorgeous. Brooke Shields was born with the looks that launch ad campaigns, and, sure enough, she did her first, for Ivory Snow, at just 11 months. Fourteen years later she wriggled into jeans to declare naughtily, "Nothing comes between me and my Calvins." In between came a furor over her exposure as a 12-year-old prostitute in *Pretty Baby* and much-hyped love scenes in *The Blue Lagoon.* "The image that was projected on me was never really me," said the brainy beauty. After a four-year sabbatical at Princeton she emerged to reveal her comic chops in Broadway's *Grease* and, eventually, her own sitcom, *Suddenly Susan.* "There's a vulnerability to her encased in strength," noted pal Whoopi Goldberg. Following a short marriage to tennis ace Andre Agassi, Shields wed sitcom writer Chris Henchy in '01 and, after arduous infertility treatments, gave birth to daughter Rowan. A new sitcom was also in her plans. "One thing I have," said the ex-child star, "is longevity."

> **I'm nothing like in the movies. I'm nothing like that at home"**

# Eddie Murphy

In 1980 Eddie Murphy became, at 19, the youngest cast member ever on the promised playland of comedy, *Saturday Night Live.* He left the show four seasons later after creating some of its most indelible characterizations: a dead-on Buckwheat update ("O-tay!"); a grumpy, foam-clad Gumby ("I'm Gumby, dammit") and his ghetto-fabulous take on Mister Rogers. By then his signature grin, braying laugh and penchant for four-letter words also ruled the big screen, following back-to-back triumphs as a wisecracking convict in *48 Hrs.*, a canny con man in *Trading Places* and a rogue lawman in *Beverly Hills Cop.* It was no surprise Hollywood dubbed a comic so bankable "Money." Murphy capped off the '80s with a sequel to *Cop,* a No. 2 pop single, a film of his stand-up act aptly titled *Raw* and truly hearty partying at his 22-room New Jersey mansion. Then a switch to PG fare in the '90s with *The Nutty Professor* and *Dr. Dolittle* suggested that his life was in turnaround. He and wife Nicole Mitchell, a model, settled down in suburbia and raised five children. (He also has three from other relationships.) "The longer he is in the business," said *Dolittle* producer John Davis, "the more normal he gets." Added actor-director pal Keenen Ivory Wayans: "I don't think he misses his wild days at all."

# Dynasty

This clan of ruthless oil tycoons and spoiled, trust-fund trollops might as well have been titled *Dallas in Denver*. The patriarch, Blake Carrington (John Forsythe), spent much of his airtime refereeing catfights, including a memorable lily-pond lollapalooza between wife Krystle (Linda Evans, below right) and his vengeful ex, Alexis (Joan Collins, center—and at right). Through it all they were dressed to kill with a glittering $10,000-per-show wardrobe budget. The Collins part had originally been offered to Sophia Loren, and the 1981-89 series stood out for its bold casting. It provided the first recurring TV role for Heather Locklear. Diahann Carroll lobbied successfully to become, she said, *Dynasty*'s first "black bitch." Ex-President Gerald Ford and wife Betty did a guest gig at a 1983 gala. And Hollywood leading man Rock Hudson played the horse-breeder lover of Linda Evans in his last role, before his death in 1985 helped make the world aware of the AIDS virus.

# Knots Landing

A down-market *Dallas* spinoff, *Knots Landing* featured J.R.'s weak-kneed, alcoholic brother Gary (Ted Shackelford), who escaped the family and Southfork and relocated to the California suburbs with wife Val (Joan Van Ark, in red at right). Infidelity, the sin of choice among the power-deprived, followed them, as neighbors traded spouses like recipes. Abby (Donna Mills, far right) was resident vixen of the cul-de-sac. In the end, the underachievers of *Knots Landing* outlasted all of the *Dallas* spawn, and their cancellation in '93 after 14 seasons ended the era of the prime-time soap. Karen (Michele Lee), the most wholesome of the cast, was in all 344 episodes.

## Dallas

The real mother of all prime-time soaps and TV topic No. 1, *Dallas* lasted 13 years and appeared on the PEOPLE cover 11 times during the magazine's formative decade. A Satan in a Stetson, J.R. (Larry Hagman) was the dominant brother of the scheming, philandering Ewing clan, a veritable human oil slick. In 1980 gunfire felled him during the finale of the second season, and some 300 million viewers in 57 countries tuned in to find out "Who Shot J.R.?" in the show's third season. The answer was J.R.'s pregnant mistress (and sister-in-law) Kristin (Mary Crosby). In a classic scene (at left), a tux-clad J.R. swings at rival Cliff Barnes (Ken Kercheval), propped up by brother Bobby Ewing (Patrick Duffy).

## 1974-1984
# SEXY SOAPS

### Daytime drama got seamier and steamier when it took over after dark

## Falcon Crest

Slotted to follow *Dallas* by CBS in '81, this saga about the grasping rich switched the venal venue from the petrol patch to a Napa Valley vineyard. Jane Wyman, the Oscar-winning first wife of President Ronald Reagan, added stature as the scheming matriarch of *Falcon Crest.* Disloyal family members connived to take over the winery from heir apparent Lance Cumson, her lazy lothario grandson, played by Lorenzo Lamas (at right, with conquest du jour Laura Johnson). With gangland rubouts, drownings, explosions and earthquakes, its nine-year run featured almost less sex than violence.

## Flamingo Road

The 1981-82 dog of the *Dallas* litter, *Flamingo Road* was set in a well-to-do Florida community and gave Morgan Fairchild—a man-eater for all seasons who also adorned *Dallas* and *Falcon Crest*—her chance to headline.

# STRONG WOMEN SENSITIVE MEN

## 1974-1984

From the Supreme Court to outer space, ladies soared, while guys explored their feminine side

**Gloria Steinem** A foot soldier in the battle for women's rights, writer Gloria Steinem helped raise the consciousness of both sexes through her articles and essays, activism and advocacy. Of her tireless crusade, the cofounder of *Ms.* magazine said feminism is "a revolution and not a public-relations movement."

## Alan Alda

How did an actor who made his mark as a sarcastic, womanizing rule breaker in TV's hit series *M\*A\*S\*H* wind up as the poster boy for the sensitive-guy movement? Campaigning for the Equal Rights Amendment and sustaining a supportive marriage to photographer Arlene Weiss (47 years and counting) helped. He gracefully bore the label until the early '80s, when, he said, "it began to mean 'weak,' 'nerdy,' 'goofy' and 'geeky.'" It had its advantages, though. "When my wife gets pissed off at me," said the four-time Emmy winner, "I tell her, 'You can't get mad at me. I'm the world's most sensitive guy.'"

## Betty Ford

Just seven weeks after her husband, Gerald, became the 38th President, Betty Ford was diagnosed with breast cancer. With a frankness that would become her hallmark, she told Americans about her illness and treatment, which included a radical mastectomy. "Her forthrightness about her breast cancer saved countless lives," said her proud husband. Years later, when faced with a drug-and-alcohol addiction, she again shared her pain with the public and cofounded the Betty Ford Center, helping thousands deal with the same problems that shadowed her life. "She speaks as one recovering alcoholic to another," said Elizabeth Taylor, one of the Center's famous patients. "There are no airs about her being the First Lady." Almost grudgingly aware of her legacy, Ford conceded, "From what I read, I think I made my mark on the First Lady position."

**Phil Donahue** Decades before Bill Clinton felt anyone's pain, there was Phil Donahue. Whether he was interviewing world leaders or donning a skirt and heels for a cross-dressing show, the empathic daytime-talk host built a largely female audience that would keep him on the air for 29 years. "Phil discovered that women in the daytime are smart," said Gloria Steinem. "He took their opinion seriously."

### **Dustin** Hoffman

If playing what he called a "bad father who tried to be a good mother" in *Kramer vs. Kramer* was Dustin Hoffman's first toe dip into the shoals of feminism, *Tootsie* was his headlong plunge. Playing an actor posing as a woman to get work, Hoffman—who tested his disguise in public in full wardrobe and makeup—indulged his fascination with women. "They scare me, they comfort me, and they possess my imagination," he said. And at times his imagination ran wild. "Dustin is still glad he's got his manhood," said *Kramer* costar Meryl Streep, "but what he really wants to do is give birth."

### **Mary Tyler Moore**

She had spunk. We loved spunk. "She became this icon of a new age, this independent woman," said *The Mary Tyler Moore Show* co-creator James L. Brooks of his heroine, Mary Richards. Playing a liberated career woman, Moore not only changed the way TV looked at females but lived the role as the chair of MTM Productions. Of the character, Moore said, "She believes, as everyone can, in possibilities."

### **Barbara** Walters

Sitting next to Harry Reasoner for ABC News in 1976, Barbara Walters became the first woman to coanchor an evening newscast—and paid the price. She caught flak about her million-dollar salary and suffered the chilly Reasoner, who "didn't want a woman," she recalled. Though her debut, said Connie Chung, was "a great moment for us all," Walters was gone in less than two years. She then focused on her celeb specials, coanchored *20/20* and served as coproducer and cohost of *The View*. "It was a long, slow climb," she said. "I wasn't consciously trying to pave the way."

**Sally Ride** "Help wanted: the first American female to orbit the Earth." Five years after answering a NASA newspaper ad, astrophysicist Sally Ride rocketed to fame on June 18, 1983, completing 97 orbits aboard the Space Shuttle. Russia had sent female cosmonauts into space in 1963 and 1982, but Capt. Bob Crippen didn't have record books in mind when he chose Ride for the mission. "I was looking for the best people," he said, "and Sally filled the bill." Since her historic flight, more than 30 other U.S. women have become astronauts. "I'm proud to be a role model for girls fascinated with the space program," she said.

## Sandra Day
### O'Connor

Her appointment to the U.S. Supreme Court "was a major step in securing opportunities for women in positions of significance," said Sandra Day O'Connor, whose only job offer after graduating third in her '52 Stanford law class was as a legal secretary. She did find attorney work in the public sector and was a state appeals court judge when President Ronald Reagan (who, former National Organization for Women president Patricia Ireland said, was feeling "the pressure of the women's vote") tapped her in '81 to be the first female justice to sit on the court. (Ruth Bader Ginsburg became the second 12 years later.) O'Connor's gender made headlines, but "the power I exert on the court," she said, "depends on the power of my arguments, not on my gender."

**Michael** Landon  The unabashedly wholesome star of TV's *Little House on the Prairie* and *Highway to Heaven,* Michael Landon radiated the warmth of home, hearth and old-fashioned American values. "He coaxed us into thinking more about our relationships with family, God and one another," said *Prairie* daughter Melissa Gilbert after his death in 1991. "Thank God for reruns."

## The Fonz
Portrayed by Henry Winkler

**The character:** Playing *Happy Days'* ingratiating greaser Arthur "Fonzie" Fonzarelli, he conferred coolness on buttoned-down Richie Cunningham (Ron Howard). **Wardrobe fixture:** Black leather jacket. **Catchphrase:** "Aaaay!" **Unlikely past:** Winkler graduated from the Yale School of Drama. **Other credits:** He starred in 1974's *The Lords of Flatbush* with newcomer Sly Stallone and now directs.

# 1974-1984
# ROCKIN' ROLES

From Mork to Kojak, Luke & Laura to Miss Piggy &
Kermit, these larger-than-life characters sealed their
decade (like Gene Simmons) with a kicky kiss

## Chrissy Snow
Portrayed by Suzanne Somers

**The character:** She was the clueless blonde roommate of
John Ritter and Joyce DeWitt for five seasons on ABC's *Three's
Company.* **Trademarks:** Though nominally employed as a typ-
ist, Chrissy sported bouncy, beribboned ponytails and hot
pants. And when she giggled, she often let out a fetching
snort. Noted Somers's husband and manager, Alan Hamel:
"She's a caricature of Suzanne's outrageous traits." They're
still married after 26 years. **Follow-up acts:** Somers starred in
two other sitcoms, wrote books on food and nutrition, survived breast cancer and became the TV promoter of her own
ThighMaster fitness products.

# ROCKIN' ROLES

### E.T. The Extra-Terrestrial

**The character:** Lost and confused himself, the sensitive alien befriended a young boy who was struggling with his parents' separation. "What we relate to," said director Steven Spielberg of *E.T.*, "is the goodness inside him." **Catchphrase:** "Phone home!" **Afterglow:** His large, luminous index finger.

### Luke & Laura Portrayed by Anthony Geary and Genie Francis

**The characters:** As star-crossed lovers on the ABC soap *General Hospital,* Luke Spencer and Laura Webber Baldwin tearfully tied the knot in '81 before some 30 million viewers, unprecedented for daytime TV. "I remember my headdress poking into my head," Francis recalled. No wonder she cried.

## The Captain & Tennille
a.k.a. Daryl Dragon
and Toni Tennille

**The players:** The husband-and-wife duo headlined a popular ABC variety show. **The hits:** "Love Will Keep Us Together," "Muskrat Love" and "Do That to Me One More Time." **Ahoy there!** Dragon, who always wore a yachting cap, got his nautical nickname from Mike Love of the Beach Boys, with whom he had toured.

## Mork Portrayed by
Robin Williams

**The character:** Mork didn't look especially alien or otherworldly but played that way on TV thanks to Williams's brilliantly improvised tics and mannerisms. "He did the whole audition standing on his head," recalled *Mork & Mindy*'s creator Garry Marshall. **Catchphrase:** "Nanu nanu," Orkian for hello and goodbye. **Other spheres:** Williams went on to win an Emmy, an Oscar and five Grammys for comedy and children's albums.

## KISS a.k.a. Gene Simmons, Ace Frehley, Paul Stanley, Peter Criss

**The characters:** Onstage, these posturing, preening, greasepainted warrior rockers stuck out their tongues and tossed their hair. They were even immortalized in a TV movie, *KISS Meets the Phantom of the Park*. Offstage, the band's goofy theatrics helped sell thousands of KISS items, including comic books, makeup and lighters. **Party anthem:** 1975's "Rock and Roll All Nite." **Critical reaction:** As Paul Stanley would say later of his lavish home, "When I bring people over, I go, 'Welcome to the house that bad reviews built.'"

# ROCKIN' ROLES

## The Village People

a.k.a. Glenn Hughes, Randy Jones, Felipe Rose, Ray Simpson, Alexander Briley, David Hodo

**The characters:** This multicultural troupe of tough guys just wanted to have fun. **Heyday:** The disco era was the perfect backdrop for their breezy, gay-themed ditties—staples of venues like Manhattan's Studio 54. **Greatest hits:** "Macho Man," "Y.M.C.A.," "In the Navy."

## Kojak

### Portrayed by Telly Savalas

**The character:** As CBS's natty, streetwise Greek-American cop Theo Kojak, he deftly bent N.Y.P.D. rules to bring bad guys to justice. **Bio:** Savalas, who died in 1994, had a Columbia degree in psych and was Jennifer Aniston's godfather. **Prop:** A lollipop. **Catchphrase:** "Who loves ya, baby?" **Answer:** PEOPLE readers, who in July 1974 made Telly the magazine's first million-selling cover subject.

## C-3PO & R2-D2 Portrayed by Anthony Daniels and Kenny Baker

**The characters:** The Force was with the droid duo, a whistling robot and his fussy gold-suited companion. **Career security:** They are the only actors in all five *Star Wars* flicks and 2005's sixth. **Self-justification:** "At one point I found myself wondering if I should get a proper job," said Daniels. "Then I thought, 'Why?' I'm very fond of C-3PO."

### 'B.A.' Baracus Portrayed by Mr. T

**The character:** A fierce, bling-bearing soldier of fortune, he led NBC's *A-Team* in the fight against evildoers everywhere. **T's real name:** Laurence Tero. **Catchphrase:** "I pity the fool!" **Numbers racket:** Mr. T reappeared in 1-800-COLLECT spots.

### Donny & Marie Osmond
Portrayed by themselves

**The roles:** The squeaky-clean teenage brother-and-sister duo treated *Donny and Marie* viewers to musical entertainment fit for the whole family, even straitlaced Mormon clans like their own. "We were so young on that show," Marie once recalled. "I look at it as an education." **Trademark:** Their "She's a little bit country, he's a little bit rock and roll" schtick. Not to mention the eye-popping Bob Mackie costumes they wore on most of their shows.

### Miss Piggy & Kermit the Frog
Voiced by Frank Oz and Jim Henson

**The characters:** Only on *The Muppet Show* would a grasping diva porker claim a kindly Everyfrog as her true love. **Hallmarks:** Her fractured French— "Moi knew what moi wanted to do"—and fracturing karate chops. The couple later starred in 1979's *The Muppet Movie*. **The shocking sellout:** Miss Piggy later hawked a bacon-and-sausage breakfast for the Denny's chain.

## Sony Walkman

With a tape player you could fit in your pocket and your own headphones, music suddenly became a personal pleasure rather than a public nuisance in '79. While some continued to disturb the peace with ultra-large, ultra-loud boom boxes, the wave of the future was the Walkman. Joggers got a beat to run to, and surly teens no longer had to suffer the backseat in silence on the annual family road trip.

**Cornrows** It was a brilliant idea, conceived by Bo Derek's husband, John, and boy, did those 200 braids make waves. Bo's look in 1979's *10* knocked not only Dudley Moore off his feet but hordes of other men as well. The Bo Braid became a hot hair-salon request even as many African-Americans were put off by the actress getting credit for a look long associated with their culture.

# FADS & FASHIONS
## 1974-1984

It was the decade to get your groove on, teetering on roller skates or platforms

**CB Radio** Truckers had 10-4'ed over them for years, but when folks started using them at home, the FCC had to add 17 channels to the citizens band.

## Toe Socks

Each little piggy got his own home. Hot in 1977 (especially in the whimsical rainbow design at right), sales petered out once people realized their toes didn't need that much wiggle room after all. While they are still an occasional novelty in the U.S. today, these "gloves for the feet" continue to be a smash hit in Japan.

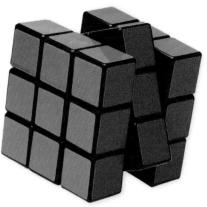

## Rubik's Cube

Named after its Hungarian creator, this brain-teasing toy made for a very frustrating 1980. Those not of tournament caliber often left the cube sitting in one of its 43.2 quintillion incomplete variations.

**Earth Shoes** This "negative-heeled" footwear was designed in Copenhagen to mimic the effect of walking in sand, which was purportedly good for posture. Marketed in the U.S. by Raymond and Eleanor Jacobs under an eco-friendly name (taken from Earth Day), they became a multimillion-dollar bonanza by the mid-'70s.

**Roller Skating** A Belgian inventor introduced the first roller skate in 1760, but it wasn't until the 1970s that they hit a critical mass. With plastic wheels making skates easier and safer, city streets across America suddenly looked like a roller derby. Skating reached its zenith in 1977, with disco music blaring from boom boxes or over the speakers at the roller rink. While you may still see a few roller skaters today, most find the more lightweight and easier to navigate Roller*blades* a cooler ride.

# FADS & FASHIONS

**Trivial Pursuit** Developed by four Canadians in 1979, this board game of random trivia ("What modern day animal is related to the prehistoric merychippus?" Answer: a horse) had a slow start, but soon everyone wanted a piece of the pie—some finding the yellow "slice" the most difficult to attain and others the brown. Twenty million units were sold in the U.S. in '84 alone, and it's still a draw among board game lovers today.

## Cabbage Patch Kids
The $27 imp-faced infants weren't just dolls, they were an addition to the family, complete with adoption papers and a birth certificate. When they were released in '83, you couldn't find one to save your life within a matter of weeks. By late '85, when supply finally caught up with demand, 50 million had been adopted.

## Valley Girls
Like, oh my God! If you were around in the early '80s, you totally remember how awesome it was to be a Val. They wore miniskirts, spent all their spare time at the mall and described a lot of things as "grody to the max." Immortalized in a song by Frank Zappa and his then 14-year-old daughter Moon Unit (earning her a Grammy nod), the phenomenon spread far beyond San Fernando. Soon the Vals were, like, everywhere. Shortly after the movie *Valley Girl* came out in 1983 (with a young Nicolas Cage in his first starring role), you'd rather be gagged with a spoon than be tarred with the by then dying label.

## Studio 54

For the bored and the beautiful, the disco epicenter of the late '70s was Manhattan's Studio 54, where regulars included (clockwise from front left) designer Halston, film producer Jack Haley Jr. with then wife Liza Minnelli, Andy Warhol and Bianca Jagger. For the few who could get past the velvet rope, it was the scene: "Boys with boys, girls with girls, girls with boys, blacks and whites, capitalists and Marxists, and everything else, all one big mix," said frequenter Truman Capote. The party for partners Steve Rubell and Ian Schrager ended in 1980, when each was sentenced to 3½ years in prison for cheating on their taxes. The magic left with them, and they sold it in '81.

### Pet Rock

This $3.95 brainchild of a California ad exec was quiet, behaved, didn't soil your rug—and sold 1.5 million. The 1975 novelty even came with a manual to teach your rock to play dead.

**Mood Ring** If it turned white, you were frustrated. Pink? Scared. Purple? Feeling amorous. In truth, the liquid crystal encased in quartz was simply heat sensitive. But no one let science ruin the fun.

### Flashdance

There was nothing innovative about the film script, nothing spectacular about the acting, but this gritty tale of a Pittsburgh welder/exotic dancer born to be a ballerina hit a nerve. Thanks to heavy video play on MTV, the soundtrack sold 700,000 copies in two weeks. Suddenly sweatshirts were being ripped unabashedly and leg warmers purchased en masse by women who wanted the **Jennifer Beals** look. The '83 blockbuster (which earned $93 million) even helped breakdancing hit the mainstream. What a feeling indeed.

# FADS & FASHIONS

## Pop Rocks

They didn't kill Mikey, as the silly rumor about the Life cereal star went—he was said to have exploded after drinking a Coke with some. Introduced in '75, the candy, which fizzed and popped in the mouth from its added carbonation, caused so much panic in parents that the FDA soon set up a hotline to assure us of its safety. The rocks are still poppin' in '04.

## Annie Hall

As Woody Allen's adorably awkward film heroine Annie Hall, Diane Keaton launched a 1977 craze for crumpled, slouchy, mannish clothes. It also became the actress's signature look. "I feel most comfortable that way," said the body-shy star, who had dated the director before the Oscar-winning movie was shot.

## Platform Shoes

Take a wrong turn and you'd suffer a terrible sprained ankle, but you'd be tall and funky before the fall. These sky-high wonders, which became a fixture by 1975, were worn by everyone from John Travolta in *Saturday Night Fever* to KISS and Elton John, whose multiple pairs were as much a staple of his '70s concerts as his trademark glasses. Not an advisable look for the balance-impaired.

## Streaking

What better way to celebrate the sexual revolution than to air your differences? The nudity craze was mostly limited to campuses, but others, like this April Fool's 1974 streaker, preferred more revered venues, like the Supreme Court. The very next day, Oscar viewers memorably caught sight of another dashing past a bemused David Niven.

# Designer Jeans

At about $35, they cost twice the price of Levi's, but with the right pair of Gloria Vanderbilt or Jordache jeans, a girl had instant status. Calvin Klein shot to the top of the denim game in '81, selling 15 million pairs after a 15-year-old Brooke Shields vowed in sultry ads that nothing came between her and her Calvins.

### The Dorothy Hamill

Ah, the wedge. Popularized by figure skater **Dorothy Hamill,** who was America's sweetheart after winning the gold medal at the '76 Olympics, the cut, which was first created by Vidal Sassoon's Trevor Sorbie in 1974, became a winner too. Suddenly every young girl was walking around with the aerodynamic do. But faster than you could say "triple salchow" they grew it out, perhaps realizing that while the cut was cute on Hamill, it did few favors for anyone else.

# ICONS

It was the heyday of a princess, two Michaels (Jackson and Jordan), *The Simpsons* and the Clintons and, sadly, the time we learned about AIDS and mourned Ryan White

## Princess Diana

Shy Di? A myth. Sly Di was more like it. At 19, when she first blinked for the paparazzi, Diana Spencer was unsophisticated if canny—always listening, watching, learning. By 1985, when she twirled with John Travolta at the White House, HRH the Princess of Wales had transformed herself from an ex-nanny novice to a knockout poised to rock the royals to their archaic core. While her endless travails and unhappy marriage vexed her staid in-laws, the world was captivated—by her beauty, her warmth, the way she mothered William and Harry and the conviction she brought to her many charities. Following Diana's 1992 separation and subsequent divorce from Charles, she lost her royal title but became what Tony Blair dubbed "the people's princess." Her tragic sudden death at 36 in 1997, in a Paris car crash with lover Dodi Fayed, was "perhaps a closing chapter for the monarchy," her biographer Andrew Morton wrote in PEOPLE. "The brightest light in the royal firmament has been snuffed out. We shall not see her like again."

# Michael Jackson

He was thrilling even as a kid, a confident, preternaturally talented 11-year-old singer fronting his four older brothers, as the Jackson Five rose to define '70s Motown pop with hits like "ABC" and "I'll Be There." Come the '80s, the loose-limbed dervish and his silky "moonwalk" ruled the world. His own album, *Thriller*, with megatunes like "Billie Jean" and "Beat It," made Michael Jackson at 24 the biggest-selling solo artist ever. "Jackson is in the air everywhere," said TIME of the self-proclaimed King of Pop, already an eccentric given to accessorizing his trademark sequined glove with a surgical mask (and frequent plastic surgery). Even before a brief, perplexing marriage to Lisa Marie Presley, things had begun to go from odd to tawdry. In 1993 Jackson was accused of molesting a 13-year-old boy (charges were later dropped, after a reported $20 million settlement), and in 1996 he suddenly married his dermatologist's assistant Debbie Rowe, who bore him a son and a daughter "as a present," he said after their discreet 1999 divorce. Repeated erratic behavior and reports of substance abuse put his career on the skids by late 2003, when he was charged with molesting a 13-year-old boy at his opulent Neverland ranch. Facing seven felony counts, his reputed $750 million fortune reportedly in ruins, Jackson angrily proclaimed his innocence as he moonwalked atop his SUV outside the courthouse. The bizarre spectacle was both maddening and sad. "This may be his last dance," mused one associate, though many, like producer Gary Pudney, who had worked with Jackson, hoped it wasn't. After all, Pudney said, "he's one of the world's greatest entertainers of all time."

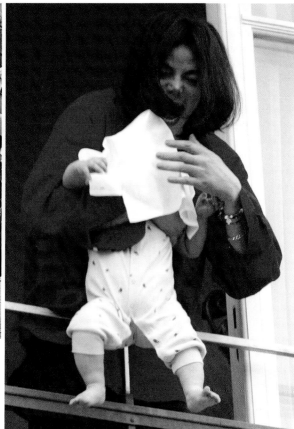

On public outings (above in 2001) Jackson kept daughter Paris, now 5, and son Prince Michael I, 6, under veil. In 2002 he caused a furor by dangling then 8-month-old son Prince Michael II over the railing of a fourth-floor balcony in Berlin.

We used to be supporters of Michael, but we don't know what to think anymore. It sure seems like something just isn't right at Neverland"
—fan Neil Dipaola

# Madonna

For two decades she put the M in MTV. Madonna Louise Veronica Ciccone, the most compellingly watchable, reliably controversial performer of her generation, helped invent the medium by reinventing herself, video by video. The coy bride with the "Boy Toy" belt in 1984's "Like a Virgin" morphed by 2000 into the ghetto-fabulous techno cowgirl of "Music." All the while she wowed adoring "wannabes" with 30-odd Top 10 singles, tasseled bras, first hubby Sean Penn, middling flicks, two kids, yoga, Kabbalah and now a quasi-Brit accent picked up from her current husband, filmmaker Guy Ritchie. The only constants? Nerves of steel and muscles to match. Britney, Christina, take note: For blondes with ambition, this is the gold standard.

# The Clintons

The most turbulent U.S. Presidency in decades began almost the minute he arrived from Arkansas in 1993, but darned if Bill Clinton and wife Hillary didn't deflect some of the glare of scandal with their laid-back, just-folks charm. He scarfed Big Macs and played the sax; she suffered through bad hair days and boogied to Fleetwood Mac at two inaugural galas. Even most foes agreed that they were model parents to daughter Chelsea, who grew out of her braces and into a poised student at Stanford (and Oxford). Astonishingly, the family remained intact after the Monica Lewinsky debacle. Hillary became a senator (and bestselling author), sparking rumors of a second Clinton in the White House. Bill, in demand on the lecture circuit and as a policy wonk, slimmed down with the South Beach Diet, polished his own memoir and was contentedly a man with a plan: "To stay out of trouble and be useful, and stay out of Hillary's hair."

> **I'm like one of those Baby Huey dolls. You punch 'em, and they come back up**
> —Bill Clinton

# Cindy Crawford

It was not just her famous mole that conquered the modeling mountain. Cindy Crawford offered more sumptuous curves than her waiflike peers and had a high school valedictorian's head for business that made her an $18 million-a-year brand name. Between ad campaigns, exercise videos and a three-year marriage to actor Richard Gere, she brought her insider's fashion info to bear as the founding host of MTV's *House of Style*. The arrival of son Presley, now 4, and daughter Kaia, 2, with nightclub entrepreneur husband Rande Gerber, didn't slow her down; both enormously telegenic kids simply joined Mom in ads for Pepsi. Through it all she remained a supermodel without attitude, once explaining, "I'm actually a midwestern girl at heart."

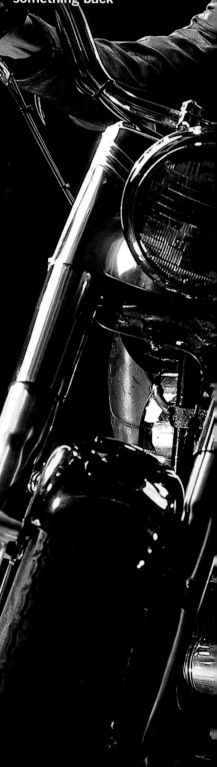

> "Everything I have gotten... the money, the family, meeting Maria, it's all because of America. I want to give something back"

# Whitney Houston

"It will take an act of Congress to keep this woman from becoming a megastar," PEOPLE predicted in '85. Indeed. Whitney Houston had flawless looks and a voice as powerful as it was beautiful—"all the credentials," in the words of cousin Dionne Warwick. And her mom, Cissy, was also a star. Whitney, signed at 19 by Clive Davis, rewarded him with what was then the bestselling debut album ever. Her second in '87 produced seven No. 1 hits, surpassing a record shared by the Beatles and the Bee Gees. Her big-screen introduction in 1992, *The Bodyguard,* was a blockbuster with a monster soundtrack. Her marriage that year to hip-hop bad boy Bobby Brown was not as well received. Yet through jail stints, trips to rehab and a heap of negative press, the couple remained together. Proud mom Whitney hints at one day passing her torch to a third generation, preteen daughter Bobbi Kristina. "You can always tell a singer by the way they hold a microphone, and she holds that mike with confidence," said Houston. "She's a little diva-in-training."

# Arnold Schwarzenegger

Who knew? He arrived on these shores in 1968 with $20, bulging biceps and a thick Austrian accent. Hardly the makings of a movie star. Then came tailor-made roles like Conan, Predator and the Terminator, and bodybuilder Arnold Schwarzenegger was relaunched as Ah-nold, the highest paid actor in Hollywood. The mystique only grew with his $25 cigars, $100,000 Hummers and bipartisan marriage to JFK's niece Maria Shriver. The ultimate jaw-dropper? The self-made Republican, after defusing charges of groping on the set, wound up as governor of California. As *Terminator 3* director Jonathan Mostow put it, "Underestimating Arnold is a mistake."

# The Simpsons

They haven't aged a day since their tube-changing debut in 1987, but otherwise the bickering, bug-eyed, chinless Simpsons (father Homer, mother Marge, 10-year-old Bart, 8-year-old Lisa and baby Maggie) more aptly convey real life than any flesh-and-blood sitcom family. "They're unrepressed and do naughty things," explained the FOX cartoon's creator Matt Groening, who named Homer and Marge after his own parents. They're "lovable," he added, "in a mutant sort of way." The ill-mannered Bart (an anagram for "brat") rattled some schoolteachers, who early on banned T-shirts bearing Bartisms like EAT MY SHORTS, but in May 2005 *The Simpsons* will unseat *The Adventures of Ozzie & Harriet* as the longest-running comedy in TV history.

# Michelle Pfeiffer

She rose into the pantheon of screen sex goddesses in '89 playing the seductive chanteuse in *The Fabulous Baker Boys*. Three years later those sapphire eyes and perfectly pouty lips peeked through a leather mask as she shook Michael Keaton's belfry as the Catwoman in *Batman Returns*. "The way my mouth curls and my nose tilts," Michelle Pfeiffer once quipped, "I should be cast as Howard the Duck." False if becoming modesty. This definitive American beauty proved her reach with a mix of gritty and glamorous roles including a single mom seduced by the devil in *The Witches of Eastwick*, the frizzy-haired, gum chomper in *Married to the Mob* and a weary waitress in *Frankie & Johnny*. In '93 Pfeiffer adopted daughter Claudia Rose and brought ubiquitous TV writer-producer David E. Kelly to the altar. Less than a year later, they welcomed son John. In the words of Rob Reiner, who directed Pfeiffer in *The Story of Us*, "It's amazing there could be one person with all these attributes. And unbelievably beautiful. There is no one quite like Michelle Pfeiffer."

# Mel Gibson

He was PEOPLE's very first Sexiest Man Alive in 1985 and deservedly so. With those mesmerizing baby blues, Mel Gibson became a box office force in roles like the vengeful postapocalyptic moralist in *Mad Max*, the half-cracked cop in *Lethal Weapon* and the blue-faced, butt-baring revolutionary in *Braveheart*, an epic that earned him director and producer Oscars. A return to Catholicism calmed his hard-partying past and inspired the father of seven to risk $25 million on the controversial film *The Passion of the Christ*. The chronicle of Christ's final hours grossed nearly $300 million in its first month. "Mel puts on no airs and makes no apologies," said admiring colleague Ron Howard. "He is who he is."

# Whoopi Goldberg

She nabbed an Oscar nomination in 1986 for her first film, *The Color Purple*, playing the subservient wife of an abusive philanderer. Yet with a name like Whoopi Goldberg (born Caryn Johnson, she pieced together a more memorable moniker from some distant relatives and, yes, the cushion), she was destined for funnier business. Five years later she won a Best Supporting Actress Oscar as a big-mouthed medium in 1990's *Ghost*. But it was donning a habit as a feisty faux-nun in the high-grossing *Sister Act* that turned Goldberg into a player. "She's talked herself into many roles," said Bill Duke, her director in the sequel. "She's had to deal with the you-don't-look-like-a-leading-lady syndrome in a system that's designed to recognize people who are her opposites." In 1994 she became the first female solo host of the Academy Awards and was invited back for that impossible gig three times since. Going on to produce *Hollywood Squares* as well as her own sitcom, Goldberg has made more than a quirky name for herself over the years. "I got lucky," the single grandma of three has said of her success. "But the fact that I'm still here means I was talented on top of it."

# Tom Cruise

With just one slide across that hardwood floor in *Risky Business*, Hollywood had a new hunk. And while the teenage fans who covered their lockers with his pictures would have been happy if Tom Cruise played every role in a pair of white skivvies and a button-down shirt like he did in that '83 breakthrough, he turned out to look equally great in dressier clothes (and more demanding roles). A flight suit, a naval uniform, a vampire cape, even, most recently, a samurai robe. His personal life was as hard to ignore as his screen presence. No couple dazzled on the red carpet like Cruise and wife Nicole Kidman. But after 10 years the couple, who have two children, called it quits. Not that the star can't light up a room or a screen on his own. As his *Jerry Maguire* costar Jay Mohr reminds us, "You can't exactly fold sweaters at the Gap with that smile."

"It's never been for the money, and it's never been for the cheers. If you don't believe me, then just watch. Because one minute I'll be there, and the next minute I'll be gone"

# Michael Jordan

Everyone wanted to be like Mike. And why not? His tongue-wagging, gravity-defying sorcery redefined the way basketball is played and had admirers—and opponents—straining for superlatives. "He is God disguised as Michael Jordan," said longtime rival Larry Bird. Besides leading the Chicago Bulls to six NBA titles in eight years and winning Olympic gold with the U.S. Dream Team in '84, '92 and '96, Jordan was a dominant force off the court as well. In 1985, his rookie year, Nike sold 2.3 million Air Jordans, launching him on his career as the premier brand name in sports merchandising and earning him an estimated $50 million a year. But tragedy struck in 1993 when his father was murdered, and he retired from the sport he loved. "I reached my pinnacle," he said. "Everyone has to make the decision at some point to move forward, away from games." It didn't last. In 1994 he tried a new game, baseball in the Chicago White Sox farm system, but struck out and returned to basketball. He played with the Bulls for a few seasons, then joined the Washington Wizards in 2000, first in the front office, then on-court, before (finally?) retiring in 2003. After a brief separation in 2002 from his wife, Juanita, with whom he has three children, Jordan resolved to save his family. "Things will work out in the long run," he vowed. They always have.

# Demi Moore

Contrary to her name, Demi Moore does nothing halfway. "I am very ambitious and very driven," the whiskey-voiced brunette conceded early on. "I want stardom." In 1987 she nailed it, eloping to Vegas with *Moonlighting*'s bad-boy heartthrob Bruce Willis. By taking "out of circulation," as PEOPLE reported, "one very active Hollywood bachelor," Moore went from Brat Pack actress (*St. Elmo's Fire, About Last Night*) to red-carpet establishment. Then—with blockbusters like *Ghost* and *Indecent Proposal* and self-promoting nude *Vanity Fair* covers—she briefly eclipsed Willis, earning a record-breaking $12.5 million paycheck for *Striptease*. After the 1998 breakup of her marriage, Moore decamped to Hailey, Idaho, and turned full-time to raising her three daughters. But, as *Ghost* director Jerry Zucker put it, "there is such a short list of people who the camera loves and can act. Demi has that thing—and she should be out there doing it." Lured out of retirement for 2003's *Charlie's Angels: Full Throttle,* she ditched anonymity and returned to unlikely power coupledom with the 15-years-younger Ashton Kutcher.

# Kevin Costner

He made the backseat of a limo a steamy destination for adventurous lovers in *No Way Out,* then turned toenail-painting into foreplay in the baseball charmer *Bull Durham.* But Kevin Costner had ambitions beyond just portraying onscreen studs. Taking himself out of the running for such blockbusters as *Presumed Innocent* and *The Hunt for Red October,* he spent 18 months putting together what was to become his masterwork. *Dances with Wolves,* the affecting Civil War epic he directed and starred in, turned Costner into the darling of the 1991 Oscars: *Wolves* won seven out of the 12 awards for which it was nominated, including Best Picture and Best Director. Costner never again equaled that triumph, but he chose projects that spoke more to his heart than to any commercial potential. "He's always known what's right for him, what's really important—rather than what others think is important," said Lawrence Kasdan, who directed Costner's famously cut coffin scene in *The Big Chill.* On the top of his list? His four children and fiancée Christine Baumgartner. "Experiencing your family," he said, "that you can never put a price on."

# Meg Ryan

With her mop of tousled blonde hair and impish smile, Meg Ryan has long been Hollywood's poster girl next door, the embodiment of wholesome sex appeal. But it was her feigned orgasm at a crowded deli in *When Harry Met Sally* that made her fame, and four years later she solidified her status as the queen of cute with Nora Ephron's follow-up script, *Sleepless in Seattle*. "I'd never thought of myself that way," said Ryan, who later pushed her dramatic mettle as a heroin addict in *The Doors* and an alcoholic in *When a Man Loves a Woman*. Still, romantic flicks were the mainstay for Ryan, who married her *Innerspace* and *D.O.A.* costar Dennis Quaid in 1991 after helping him kick a cocaine habit. The couple, who share a son, Jack Henry, divorced in 2001, after Ryan's fling with Russell Crowe. "She's quite a formidable presence," said Tom Hanks, a three-time costar. "She's not a little wisp of a blondie."

# Jodie Foster

She began acting at age 3, in a Coppertone commercial, and got her first Oscar nomination at 14 as an underage hooker in *Taxi Driver*. Still, the Yale alum (cum laude) felt so emotionally drained playing the party girl turned rape victim in *The Accused* that she nearly gave up acting for grad school. "No one would ever hear from me again," she said. In fact, the world heard from her soon thereafter in her 1989 Oscar acceptance speech for *The Accused* and then again, three years later, after her second Oscar for *The Silence of the Lambs*. The parts weren't always so challenging, and Foster began to direct with 1991's *Little Man Tate*. "This is not a business that is kind to women," observed the mom of two. "But it needs them."

# Ryan White

At his death in 1990, Ryan White, 18, was America's kid, a human face for AIDS at a time of bigotry against its victims. White, a hemophiliac who contracted HIV from blood-clotting products at 12, was banned from his school in Kokomo, Indiana. After his mother sued to have him reinstated, the community sent hate mail, dumped garbage on the Whites' lawn, even fired a bullet into their home. Ryan spoke out with courageous eloquence and, with help from Elton John and Phil Donahue, he moved across the state to Cicero. "People would back away from me on the street," he recalled. "Maybe I would have been afraid of AIDS too, but I wouldn't have been mean about it." Following White's death, Congress passed the Ryan White CARE Act, which funds AIDS treatment. "He gave us understanding and compassion," said White's minister, Bud Probasco. "He was a little boy, but he taught us all about big hearts."

# Harrison Ford

We already knew he could play tough. His hardheaded Han Solo and whip-wielding maverick Indiana Jones rank among Hollywood's most bankable heroes. Then Harrison Ford showed his more sensitive side, getting an Oscar nod as an undercover cop with a soft spot for an Amish woman in 1985's *Witness* and extending his range as a brain-damaged lawyer in *Regarding Henry*. While we welcomed Ford's heavier fare, he wasn't about to slip off and do indie flicks. "I don't feel any lack of noble purpose if I do a film that's commercial," he said, referring to signature parts like the archeology prof adventurer he played for a third time in 1989, with a fourth installment due in 2006. His 18-year marriage to screenwriter Melissa Mathison having ended in 2001, he is now dating Calista Flockhart, 22 years his junior. "I'm in love," he said. "I was not surprised that I was able to fall in love, but I'm very grateful."

**" I'm like old shoes. I've never been hip. I think the reason I'm still here is that I was never enough in fashion that I had to be replaced by something new"**

**The Cosby Show** In a comfortable Brooklyn brownstone, obstetrician Cliff Huxtable (Bill Cosby), his lawyer wife and their five charming kids (among them Keshia Knight Pulliam) offered a gentle look at family life. At its peak, nearly half of U.S. sets were tuned in on Thursday nights to hear Cos deliver his homespun homilies in Technicolor sweaters.

**Family Ties** The ideal sitcom star for the Reagan era, Michael J. Fox stole the show as Alex P. Keaton, yuppie Republican son of ex-hippie folks (Michael Gross, left, and Meredith Baxter Birney, right). Sure, Alex was arrogant, but viewers—and ditzy sis Mallory (Justine Bateman)—loved him anyway.

**Cheers** Everybody knew their names: owner Sam (Ted Danson) and waitress Diane (Shelley Long), who fell in love while tending to a top-notch cast of tipplers (and trivia freak Cliffie) on tap at a Boston pub.

**Seinfeld** It was a show about nothing—except Festivus ("the festival for the rest of us"), close talkers, re-gifters, Dolores and dozens of other details from the lives of four self-absorbed Manhattan singles (including **Julia Louis-Dreyfus**). Living up to a flinty motto—"No Hugging, No Learning"—creators **Jerry Seinfeld** and Larry David ended the nine years with the gang in jail. Not that there's anything wrong with that.

**Roseanne** It was a groundbreaking concept: an honest—and honestly funny—view of blue-collar America. Stand-up comic **Roseanne Barr** (with **John Goodman**) pulled no punches exploring alcoholism, divorce, homosexuality and unemployment. Her volatile temperament stirred a buzz offscreen as well.

### Murphy Brown

**Candice Bergen** was "Murph," the sarcastic, hard-charging, secretary-shredding host of the *60 Minutes*-like news show *FYI*. But in 1992 single mom Brown and her newborn son Avery became news themselves when then Vice President Dan Quayle, in a speech on family values, accused her of "mocking the importance of fathers by bearing a child alone and calling it just another lifestyle choice."

# 1985-1994
# MUST-SEE
# SITCOMS

What was all the yada yada yada about? Single mom Murph and kindly dad Cos, a smooth-talking yuppie and a tart-tongued 'domestic goddess.' Cheers!

## Regis Philbin & Kathie Lee Gifford

**Claim to fame:** Genially dyspeptic (him) and generally ditzy (her) hosts of ABC's *Live! with Regis & Kathie Lee,* they began each day with 15 minutes of unscripted observations and bickering before guests arrived.

**Schmooze topics:** You name it. Traffic; Gifford's marriage to footballer Frank; their kids Cody and Cassidy; Philbin's mother-in-law, Ethel "Hello, Let's Eat!" Senese; fixing up Gelman (the show's executive producer); Gifford's inner thighs; Philbin's kidney stones; Frank's nude sleepwalking; what to have for lunch . . .

**Grating soundbite:** "Reeeege!"

# 1985-1994
# OVER THE TOP!

Like a sex doc and the film *Croc,* Reege was too much but H-O-T (thanks, Vanna)

# OVER THE TOP!

## Vanna White

**Claim to fame:** Since 1982 she has been Pat Sajak's evening-gowned letter turner and mute sidekick on *Wheel of Fortune*.
**Breaking the silence:** Her 1987 autobiography, *Vanna Speaks!*, was a bestseller. Her TV movie *Goddess of Love* (she played V-E-N-U-S) didn't fare as well.
**Her A for effort:** "My job is not all that difficult. But I do have to know the entire alphabet."

## Crocodile Dundee

**Real name:** Paul Hogan
**Claim to fame:** His two film blockbusters limned the essential Aussie: a garrulous bloke in a weird hat, ever ready with a hunting knife and a "G'day, mate."
**And lest we forget:** In ads for his country's tourism board, he promised to "throw another shrimp on the barbie."

## Milli Vanilli

**Real names:** Rob Pilatus (left) and Fabrice Morvan
**Claim to fame:** From the get-go in Germany, they knew what was important. "To be a star you have to have special hair," explained Pilatus, and for two years the pair tossed their shoulder-length tress extensions through hot singles like "Girl You Know It's True."
**Oops, not that true:** In 1990 it was revealed that they lip-synched during concerts and hadn't sung a note of their album. Their best new artist Grammy was rescinded, and fans who had bought records got $3 reimbursements.
**Sad coda:** In 1998 Pilatus died of a drug and alcohol overdose in a hotel near Frankfurt.

## Judge Wapner

**First name:** Joseph

**Claim to fame:** From the bench of TV's *The People's Court,* the former L.A. Superior Court judge presided over 4,600 small-claims cases brought before him by livid neighbors and feuding relatives. The ardent baseball fan once went to Anaheim Stadium to mediate a manager-player dispute for the California Angels.

**Man bites dog:** Put his robe back on in 1997 for *Judge Wapner's Animal Court* on Animal Planet.

## Pee-wee Herman

**Real name:** Paul Reubens

**Claim to fame:** After scoring in theaters with *Pee-wee's Big Adventure,* the manic man-child with the tight suit and sly humor made the psychedelic TV world of *Pee-wee's Playhouse* the hip place for kids and adults to be on Saturday mornings.

**Claim to infamy:** Arrested in '91 for indecent exposure in a Florida adult movie house.

# OVER THE TOP!

## Macaulay Culkin

**Claim to fame:** His scream in *Home Alone* outwitted bumbling burglars and drew fans around the world.

**Payoff:** *Home* was the third-biggest-grossing film in history at the time; his allowance was reportedly $5 a day.

**He's *baaack:*** As a murderous transvestite in 2003's *Party Monster.*

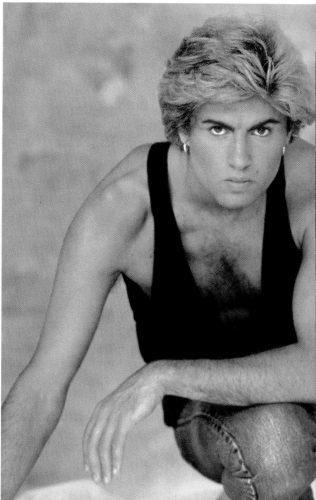

## Robin Leach

**Claim to fame:** This globe-trotting, trumpet-voiced British host led viewer voyeurs into Adnan Khashoggi's gilded bathroom and Cher's shoe closet on *Lifestyles of the Rich and Famous.*

**Signature line:** "Champagne wishes and caviar dreams."

**All in a day's work:** "Nothing gets my journalistic juices flowing more than a seaside chalet, the mention of a private jet or room service in St. Tropez."

## Boy George

**Real name:** George O'Dowd
**Claim to fame:** He merged hippie and Hasidic-like wear as the colorfully androgynous crooner of Culture Club's "Do You Really Want to Hurt Me."
**Anticlimax:** Appeared in Rosie O'Donnell's stage bio of him, the '03 Broadway bomb *Taboo*.

## Richard Simmons

**Claim to fame:** The flamboyant ex-fattie was already a fitness guru when he got America moving with bestselling *Sweatin' to the Oldies* exercise videos. With fans (he phoned 50 daily), he would melt into heartfelt tears at the drop of a pound.
**Who are you wearing?** The proud owner of just one pair of pants was rarely seen in anything but a tank top and short shorts (sequins optional), even when sparring with David Letterman.
**Food for thought:** "Put your fork down and like yourself."

## George Michael

**Real name:** Georgios Kyriacos Panayiotou
**Claim to fame:** The blond half of Brit duo Wham! implored listeners to "Wake Me Up Before You Go-Go." His solo hit "I Want Your Sex" was widely banned.
**No-no:** Arrested in 1998 by an undercover cop for committing a lewd act in the men's room of an L.A. park.

# OVER THE TOP!

## Pamela Anderson

**Claim to fame:** Five seasons in flaming red as New Agey *Baywatch* babe C.J. Parker.
**Married name (1995-98):** Lee
**Assets:** Displayed them in *Playboy* and on *Home Improvement* before hitting the beach. In regular rotation ever since.
**Career plan:** "I love the dumb-blonde image. Then I have nothing to live up to. I can only surprise people."

## Debbie Gibson

**Claim to fame:** As a squeaky-clean teen piano prodigy, she penned the bubblegum anthems "Shake Your Love" and "Foolish Beat" in her Long Island garage.
**Pure enough for parody:** Mojo Nixon satirized her image in "Debbie Gibson Is Pregnant with My Two-Headed Love Child."
**Encore:** As Deborah, has kept busy on Broadway with roles in *Les Miz, Beauty and the Beast* and *Cabaret.*

Menudo, meet Mickey. Ricky Martin (far right) and his bandmates in Disney's domain in 1988.

## Menudo

**Claim to fame:** A Puerto Rican ensemble phenom, it systematically replaced its pubescent boy members when they turned 16.
**Most famous alum:** Ricky Martin.
***Qué pasa?*** Martin went on to "Livin' la Vida Loca" and "She Bangs." Others among the more than 30 Menudans emeriti have reunited periodically to tour.

## Dr. Ruth

**Real name:** Born Karola Ruth Siegel to German Holocaust victims, she grew up in Switzerland.
**Claim to fame:** TV/radio sex therapist; author of some 20 books; size didn't matter (she's 4'7").
**Mantra for mankind:** "Have good sex!"

## Fabio

**Last name:** Lanzoni
**Claim to fame:** He was the cover boy on more than 300 romance novels and spokesguy for I Can't Believe It's Not Butter!
**Groupies:** Primarily grannies, though he later dated Larissa Meek of *Average Joe: Hawaii*.
**Last seen:** Cameos in *Zoolander, Bubble Boy* and *Dude, Where's My Car?*

# SCANDALS

From power seats to penthouse suites, these public offenders
proved the bigger they were, the harder they fell

# O.J. Simpson

Simpson's day in court with lawyers
Robert Shapiro (left) and Cochran.

## In the trial of the century, a fallen idol scored a startling upset win

"If it doesn't fit, you must acquit." So Johnnie Cochran, the captain of Simpson's legal Dream Team, advised the jury after his former NFL star client struggled into gloves found in the 1994 murder investigation of his ex-wife Nicole Brown Simpson and her friend Ron Goldman. After a yearlong trial, he was clamorously acquitted. Later he moved to Miami with his two children by Nicole but found himself virtually unemployable as he tried to raise the $33.5 million a 1997 civil suit awarded the victims' families. Even his Heisman Trophy went on the auction block, and he never delivered on his quest to find "the real killers."

# SCANDALS

## Jessica Hahn, Tammy Faye & Jim Bakker

### Their lust and greed cost them an evangelical empire

A tryst with church secretary Jessica Hahn buried the multimillion-dollar Praise the Lord ministry built by Jim Bakker and his wife, but the unholy trinity survived. Jim served five years for fraud and heads a small L.A. church. Tammy, diagnosed with inoperable lung cancer, starred on *The Surreal Life*. Hahn got a new nose, teeth, breasts and a *Playboy* spread.

After Hahn (top) went public in '87, Tammy and Jim shed some tears, divorced and found new spouses.

## Woody Allen, Mia Farrow & Soon-Yi
### An adoptive family trauma

After 12 years with Mia Farrow, Woody Allen, 56, shockingly took up with her daughter Soon-Yi Previn, 21, in 1992. His defense? "The heart wants what it wants." Surviving child-abuse charges and a custody fight for his three kids with Farrow, Allen wed Previn in '98 and adopted two daughters.

## Nancy Kerrigan & Tonya Harding
### A whack job tried to unseat an ice princess

"Why me? Why?" It was a fair question for Nancy Kerrigan (left) to ask after a man walked up to her and clubbed her leg in 1994. Rival Tonya Harding knew the answer. But her plot, with ex-hubby Jeff Gillooly, to sabotage Kerrigan failed: Nancy made the U.S. Olympic team and won a silver medal, while Tonya was banned for life from U.S. figure skating and served three years probation. Kerrigan went on to tour in *Champions on Ice*. Harding is slugging it out in a new arena. After facing Paula Jones in a *Celebrity Boxing* match in 2002, she turned pugilist.

# Leona Helmsley

## How tax evasion and bad labor relations dethroned the Queen of Mean

It was the ultimate payback when Leona Helmsley, the woman who ruled her real estate empire with an icy cruelty and declared taxes were for "the little people," was found guilty in 1989 of bilking the government of more than $1 million. Despite a net worth in the billions and holdings that included Manhattan's Helmsley Palace Hotel and the Empire State Building, Leona and husband Harry billed such personal expenses as a $1 million pool house and $468 in underwear to their business. Harry was declared mentally unfit to stand trial (he died in 1997), but Leona served 18 months in a federal prison. Her legal problems weren't over though. Recently two business associates sued her, saying they were fired because they were gay. The court cases cost her more than $1 million, but the queen's means were still in 10 figures.

# Gary Hart & Donna Rice
## An ill-timed joyride on a yacht sank a presidential candidate's political fortunes

Daring the press to "put a tail on me" was Gary Hart's first mistake. Boarding a boat called *Monkey Business* in 1987 with would-be model-actress Donna Rice was his second—and last. The married Democratic senator, whose career had been dogged with allegations of womanizing, denied any impropriety, telling *Nightline*'s Ted Koppel "the woman in question" had simply "dropped into my lap. I chose not to dump her off." Rice mostly kept quiet, did some smirky commercials for No Excuses jeans, then embraced evangelical Christianity and wed a businessman. A respected statesman and international lawyer, Hart now gets his adrenaline rush penning thrillers under the nom de plume John Blackthorn.

# Anita Hill & Clarence Thomas

## This 'he said, she said' saga rocked the political and sexual landscape

In 1991, when Anita Hill testified about sexual innuendos allegedly made by her former boss Clarence Thomas in hearings on his nomination to the Supreme Court, she was called a liar and forced to recount Thomas's humiliating jest about a pubic hair on a Coke can. She may have lost the battle—Thomas survived what he called a "high-tech lynching," won Senate confirmation and now sits on the high court—but she won the war. Within a year corporations across the country stepped up efforts to educate employees about sexual harassment, and the Equal Employment Opportunity Commission (where Hill and Thomas had worked together) logged a record 9,920 complaints. Now a Brandeis law prof, Hill titled her 1997 memoir *Speaking Truth to Power*.

## Oliver North
### Was he the good soldier or a Rambo run amok?

Accused in 1987 of funding Nicaraguan rebels with the sale of U.S. arms to Iran, the telegenic Marine was the star of the Iran-Contra hearings. Convicted on three counts, Oliver North got the convictions overturned on appeal. A senatorial bid failed, but he scored with a bestselling book, speakings gigs at up to $25,000 a pop and a job as host of *War Stories with Oliver North* on Fox News Channel.

The golden age of the Trumps ended when Marla Maples (below right) told a tabloid The Donald was "the best sex I ever had."

# Donald Trump, Ivana Trump & Marla Maples

## Scenes from a marriage— and a divorce—of excess

Like everything Trumpian, the 1991 demise of the 13-year marriage of Ivana and Donald was "yooge." She wanted half his supposed $5 billion but settled for $10 million, a $12 mil mansion and custody of their three kids. Close to bankruptcy by '93, Donald wed Marla Maples and they had a child before divorcing in '99. All now single, Ivana heads her own companies, Marla is an actress and Trump moonlights as über-boss on *The Apprentice*.

**Christian Lacroix Pouf**

He was the anti-Armani—with a solo debut collection so daringly fun that anyone with $10,000 to spare in '87 popped for an original pouf skirt. Or, for the rest of us, a knockoff. Still, even the French designer himself knew the deal: "To be in style," he said, "is to be out of style one second later." By '88 it went poof.

# 1985 FADS & FASHIONS 1994

If you sported a Swatch, swiveled in your Pouf, ventured Bon Jovi hair and dug WrestleMania, you truly lived the era

## WrestleMania

Real or fake? Such was the question when **Hulk Hogan**, **Rowdy Roddy Piper** and their musclebound pals took to the ring. Alas, the "sport" was choreographed and the endings fixed, but that didn't deter the millions glued to the campy bouts, some at extortionate pay-per-view premiums. "It's hip. It's exciting. It's America," pronounced fan Andy Warhol.

## Swatch

One in every color? Impossible! This too-many-to-choose-from line of eye-catching plastic time-pieces was designed by a pair of Swiss watchmakers to compete with cheapo brands from Japan. At just $30 a pop, every teen had one—if not six—by 1985, the year the 10 millionth Swatch rolled out. Two decades later they're still tickin'.

## Nintendo

With more than 30 million homes twiddling their thumbs on Nintendo joysticks by '91, one poll showed more kids could identify **Mario** than Mickey Mouse. The craze faded post-PlayStation in '95.

# FADS & FASHIONS

### Koosh Balls

These rubberized sea urchins were as addictive as a Rubik's Cube but not so mind-boggling. Invented by Silicon Valley engineer Scott Stillinger, who wanted to teach his kids catch with a softer ball, the toy became the hot Christmas buy of '88. Thanks to talk show host Rosie O'Donnell, who often slung them at her audience, the Koosh got another poosh in the late '90s.

### AIDS Ribbons

Stars like **Elizabeth Taylor** turned the simple twist of red into an award show staple in the early '90s, and those opting out were practically excommunicated—as noted in a memorable *Seinfeld* episode. Soon more colors hit the scene, like pink for breast cancer, purple for opposing urban violence and green for the environment.

# Showing Off Your Undies

Before girls' thongs began playing peek-a-boo out of today's low-rise jeans, tighty whities got some major air time thanks to rapper-turned-Calvin-Klein-model Mark Wahlberg, whose size-34 jeans hung off his 32-inch waist back in '92. Soon, all the boys were doing it. Why did they stop? Probably the same reason Wahlberg did. "It just wasn't that comfortable anymore," he said. "You've got to dig past your knees to reach in your pocket. And God forbid if I had to run."

# Miami Vice

Men's fashion got a facelift after Don Johnson came ashore in '84. Maybe the show's fans couldn't afford the super-fast Cigarette boats, Ferraris or women, but a pastel tee, no socks and an unstructured suit? No problem. Macy's created a *Miami Vice* section in its men's department. Aside from proving that real men can wear pink, the show turned Miami, once dubbed "God's waiting room" for all its retirees, into a tourist hotbed.

### Parachute Pants

Forget his three Grammys. M.C. Hammer's real crowning achievement was popularizing what are perhaps the silliest trousers in history. In '91 Simplicity even offered a $7.50 pattern for a do-it-yourself version.

### New Coke

If it ain't broke, don't fix it. Simple logic, but Coca-Cola execs thought they could improve on the best-selling 19th-century formula in '85. A crush of complaints led to the return of what they dubbed "Classic" Coke within 77 days.

### Scrunchies

They offered new ways for tying ponytails back in the early '90s. But Teri Garr and the like committed a multitude of fashion sins by wearing them, as noted a decade later by the more savvy on *Sex and the City*.

# FADS&FASHIONS

## Bon Jovi Hair

Giving love a bad name wasn't quite the crime **Jon Bon Jovi** made it out to be. Not compared with this hairstyle the band spread to the masses. Layered, frosted and oh-so-frizzy, both sexes had pumped up the volume by '87.

## Baby on Board

Ubiquitous in 1986, this obnoxious sign warned passing cars to take extra care on account of the precious little ones riding inside. It was quickly matched by many parodies like "Nobody on Board," "Baby Driving" and "Ex-Wife in Trunk."

**BABY ON BOARD!**
Safety 1st® puts Children 1st

## Beanie Babies

Folks first loved these cute stuffed animals in '93 for their cuddly feel and $5 price. Then the collectible frenzy began. With inventor-turned-billionaire Ty Warner's limited-release plan, Americans lost their marbles trying to collect them all.

## Cordless Phones

Static rendered them near useless early on, but in 1986 the FCC added a higher frequency, which meant less noise for cordless phones. Soon everyone was singing their praises, including opera heavy **Luciano Pavarotti**.

## Grunge

With the excess of the '80s ending in serious recession in the early '90s, fashion followed suit. Gen Xers took **Kurt Cobain**'s lead and donned a grim uniform of flannel shirts and ripped jeans.

# Madonna Wannabes

What might Halloween in the mid-'80s have been without Madonna? No mesh shirts, no jelly bracelets, lace stockings or digging in Mom's drawer for garish red lipstick. Playing dress-up became everyday life for some. Teenyboppers from coast to coast wanted to look like a virgin (and not in the pure sense). It caused an uproar among parents and school principals alike, but, as another pop icon noted—girls just wanna have fun.

# Barney

When this 6-ft. singing purple dinosaur began walking the earth, children squealed with joy, and adults cringed with utter disdain. The show, said creator Sheryl Leach, who produced Barney videos for five years before PBS gave the T-Rex a series in 1992, "has a magical simplicity to it that parents don't understand." No matter. By keeping millions of their kids occupied for hours on end, Barney turned out to be a blessed friend of the family.

## Power Rangers

Cheesy, low-budget and not particularly innovative, the *Mighty Morphin Power Rangers* nevertheless became the No. 1 morning show among the 2-to-11 bracket when it debuted in '93. Spliced with Japanese sci-fi footage, the quintet of action-hero boys and girls battled a gaggle of evil space aliens like Squatt, a "half warthog, half blueberry, with a brain the size of a peach pit." They also promoted tolerance and self-confidence, were criticized for their violence and earned $1 billion within a year.

**My life collapsed. People ran from me because suddenly it was 'Oh my God! It's over for her now!'"**
—On her split with Cruise

# 1995-2004
# ICONS

We rooted for Nicole, hailed Halle and adored *Sex* with Sarah Jessica

## Nicole Kidman

On the morning after she was named Best Actress for playing Virginia Woolf in *The Hours,* Nicole Kidman woke up to the Oscar glittering beside her bed and wondered, "How did this happen?" For the rest of the planet, the answer was obvious. Hollywood loves a good comeback story, and hers is a doozy. Once considered icy and aloof, the alabaster-skinned Australian became the nominee to root for after Tom Cruise divorced her in 2001. With her world "falling apart," Kidman eased into her new life, sharing custody with Cruise of their two children, Bella and Connor. Meanwhile she threw herself into serious work, pouring her pain into her performance in *The Hours,* followed by *Cold Mountain* and *The Human Stain.* In red carpet appearances, she evolved from eye candy to designer's dream— and recently signed on as the new face of Chanel No. 5. Kidman "has an exquisite sense of style, but more importantly she has an inherent sense of grace," observed *Moulin Rouge* director Baz Luhrmann. Added friend Sydney Pollack, director of her upcoming thriller *The Interpreter*: "It's very, very pleasing when you watch someone blossom and flower like that."

# Keanu Reeves

The enigmatic smile, that inscrutable gaze, his general air of "huh, me?"—Keanu Reeves long made a career of convincing fans (and reviewers) that he was just a ditzy dude. Then he began to dispel that perception, playing an action hero in 1994's *Speed*, and he totally retired it with his breakthrough *Matrix* series. That futuristic sci-fi trilogy left a few moviegoers scratching their heads, but there was finally recognition that Reeves himself—his first name means "cool breeze over the mountains" in Hawaiian—was not to be confused with his lightweight image as half of the dim-witted team of time-traveling teens who became slacker icons in *Bill & Ted's Excellent Adventure*. "People sometimes can't get past the performance to the person," said *Matrix* producer Joel Silver of the ever-mysterious star, a motorcycle enthusiast who plays bass in the band Dogstar—and reveals little else of his off-screen life. "He is very bright." And determined not to be pigeonholed. Post *Matrix*, Reeves reverted to a mix of quirky films and the mainstream—such as wooing Diane Keaton in *Something's Gotta Give*. "Of course he's not a flake at all," she said. "You can't be a flake and be Keanu."

# Beyoncé

It's not every day that a pop star contributes to the lexicon of the English language. But with the pervasiveness of "Bootylicious," her catchy anthem of 2001, Beyoncé Knowles landed herself not only on the *Billboard* charts but also in the *Oxford English Dictionary*. A picture of Knowles could have sufficed for the definition: Bootylicious translates as "sexually attractive." As a grade-schooler she appeared on *Star Search* with future Destiny's Child bandmates, and defeat has not since been part of her destiny. Between the group's albums and *Dangerously in Love*, Knowles's solo debut in '03, the singer has sold a total of 35 million. With her wigged-out 2002 turn as Foxxy Cleopatra in *Austin Powers in Goldmember*, Knowles added movie star to her ever-growing résumé. She is set to appear next opposite Steve Martin in a remake of *The Pink Panther*. "I want to be the first black woman to win an Oscar, a Tony and a Grammy," she once boasted. With eight Grammys already in hand, Knowles, who is dating rapper Jay-Z, is on a roll. "Beyoncé is like the Halley's comet of pop culture," said talk show host Carson Daly. "She's that powerful."

# Cameron Diaz

She loves rare steak and greasy french fries. She swears like a soldier, listens to heavy metal and punctuates her sentences with a raucous laugh. Cameron Diaz "is an extremely cool human," said Jim Carrey, her costar in *The Mask,* "despite having what normally can be character-crippling good looks." While her pulchritude couldn't go unnoticed, Diaz managed to break out of modeling and become one of Hollywood's top-paid actresses by downplaying her beauty in favor of goofy, one-of-the-guys accessibility. Likened to the legendary Carole Lombard by her *Gangs of New York* director Martin Scorsese, she shot to stardom in the giggly, gross-out smash *There's Something About Mary* and continued her reign as America's silliest, sexiest sweetheart in *The Sweetest Thing* and the two *Charlie's Angels* movies. Since summer of '03, Diaz has been globe-trotting with her pop star beau Justin Timberlake, who, like most everyone else, describes her as "a lot of fun." Observed her *Charlie's Angels* castmate Drew Barrymore: "Nobody makes decisions from their heart the way she does. Nobody is more in touch with their instincts."

# John F. Kennedy Jr.

When the single-engine Piper Saratoga that JFK Jr. was piloting plunged into the waters off Martha's Vineyard on a July night in 1999, killing him, his wife, Carolyn Bessette, and her sister Lauren, the nation reeled in sorrowful disbelief. We had known this dazzling political scion for all his 38 years: the toddler who bravely saluted his father's casket; the hunky public escort of his sister Caroline and his mother, Jackie; the free spirit who Rollerbladed shirtless in Manhattan; the determined editor of *George* magazine. Remarkably, even with the entire world watching his every step, John prided himself on "living a fairly normal life," he said. "I thank my mother for doing that." And though he was pursued by women famous and beautiful, he took his time finding one who seemed a genuine match. Despite recent unflattering portrayals of his marriage, friends say John's legacy had only just begun— that he was looking forward to fatherhood and a run for public office. "Like his father," John's uncle Ted said at the funeral, "he had every gift but length of years."

# Jennifer Aniston

"You feel like you've just been pushed out of a plane and you're in free fall," Jennifer Aniston said of her *Friends*-fueled fame. The altitude agreed with her. Flying high ever since Rachel launched The Haircut, Aniston took her character from spoiled rich girl to career woman to single working mother, making her one of the most fully evolved Friends and drawing personal comparisons to Lucille Ball and Mary Tyler Moore. "What's so weird about this show is that so much of our lives get in there," said the $1 million-per-episode Emmy winner. "It did feel like I was growing up in front of everybody." Aniston worked her quirky charm on moviegoers too, receiving solid reviews for her against-type role as a dowdy clerk in *The Good Girl*. "She's a blessed person," said *Friends* costar Matthew Perry. "But she's also worked hard." When the series ended its 10-year run, Aniston cried, then turned her focus to films and her marriage to Brad Pitt. "I never want to get stagnant and comfortable," she said. "I think change is a good thing."

# Britney Spears

She started out in pigtails, but it was soon apparent that pop princess Britney Spears was a Madonna in the making. Ditching the schoolgirl uniform she wore at 17 to promote her 13-million-selling debut album, . . . *Baby One More Time,* the former Mouseketeer opted for much racier videos and far sparser clothing. She popped up nearly naked on magazine covers and in clubs from Manhattan to Malibu while rebounding from a much-publicized breakup with 'N Sync alum Justin Timberlake. "I did party a bit, but what the hell else am I gonna do?" she wondered. That was just a warm-up for her jolting awards-ceremony smooch with Madonna herself and a Las Vegas marriage to childhood pal Jason Alexander (annulled 55 hours later). "If I mess up, I'm human," she declared. "I'm no different from anyone else my age." No different except that by 22 she had released a steamy fourth album (*In the Zone*), was embarking on a world tour and had a net worth of some $150 million. Yes, even Brit-Brit (as her mom calls her) had to admit, "I wake up, and I can't believe this is my life."

# Brad Pitt

Don't hate him because he's beautiful. The only man to be named PEOPLE's Sexiest Man Alive twice, Brad Pitt has spent his career fighting the pretty-boy label. "I'm one of those people you hate because of genetics," he once said. "It's the truth." Not exactly. He did raise heart rates—and his Hollywood profile—on a romp with Geena Davis in *Thelma & Louise,* but then he quickly opted for gutsier roles in films like *12 Monkeys* (copping him an Oscar nod). "This is not a guy who's going, 'How does this slot into my life?' " said David Fincher, his director in *Seven* and *Fight Club.* "It's more like, 'Tell me a story that makes me want to give up everything to go do it.' " Equally passionate about design, he spent two years remodeling a $13.5-million spread with *Friends* star wife Jennifer Aniston. Whether applied to his film career or side interest, a quote from architect Frank Gehry "spoke volumes" to him, Pitt said: " 'If you know where it's going, it's not worth doing.' "

# Oprah Winfrey

What constitutes clout? Money? Influence? For nearly 20 years, few have earned more of either than Oprah Winfrey. The richest female entertainer in the world was no mere talk show host. Her afternoon show became a top-rated pulpit to preach her female-friendly sermon of hope and self-empowerment. For her honesty, humor and "you go, girl!" attitude, her viewers—some 30 million of them—loved the one-time TV anchor with near religious fervor, and from Winfrey's lips to the bestseller lists went all 48 books she recommended during the original run of her on-air "book club." (Similarly, Oprah propelled frequent guest Dr. Phil, a psychologist, into his own show.) When Oprah dieted, millions dieted; when she started *O* magazine and posed for every cover, readers subscribed in droves. "As a celebrity you can make the decision to cut yourself away from the world or be part of it," said Winfrey, who involved viewers in a wide range of causes. "I chose to be a part of it. Big time." Huge, actually. With a net worth estimated at $1 billion, the once dirt-poor girl from Mississippi, the descendent of slaves, now shared multiple homes with her longtime steady beau, marketing executive Stedman Graham. But her most valuable asset remained her ability to inspire. "I woke up one morning and realized, 'Who am I to be tired?'" Winfrey recalled. "I come from a people who had no voice, no power, no money, no nothing. Now I have a position of power. I have a voice to speak to millions of people every day. So how dare I think I can stop. I can't."

# Tom Hanks

It's clear the man loves his job, but don't accuse him of being an artist. "What I like about acting is it's not working, it's pretending," said Tom Hanks. "Choosing a role is always purely an instinctual choice. It has to be an instantaneous lunge." So far he's made some remarkable leaps, winning two Oscars (for *Philadelphia* and *Forrest Gump*) and headlining critic-pleasing blockbusters like *Apollo 13* and *Saving Private Ryan*. The fact that most of his characters tend to be exemplary individuals is no accident. "The man is as nice, as honest, as professional, as personal as he seems to be," said *Gump* producer Steve Tisch. "He's an extremely talented actor, and as a human being he is what we all should aspire to be." But the actor often called Hollywood's Everyman says he's simply a regular guy trying to enjoy life with wife Rita Wilson and his four children. "Work, family, life," he said. "That's just it."

# Jennifer Lopez

She's been called Jennifer, Jenny, J.Lo, and of course she was half of that horrible, ill-fated hybrid "Bennifer." But then Jennifer Lopez has always been hard to pin down. Is she a singer? An actress? A restaurateur? Since her triumph in 1997's *Selena*, she has been all of them and more. She clicked with George Clooney in *Out of Sight*, then went on to open a Pasadena eatery, launch a fragrance, rack up $65 million in sales from her clothing line and release her third multiplatinum album, *This Is Me... Then*. "I see myself as an artist, and an artist expresses herself in different ways," said the first Latina actress to earn $12 million per film. "I don't limit myself to just doing movies or singing, because I wouldn't be fulfilled if I did." Leaving behind a storm of headlines with almost-husband-No.-3 Ben Affleck, Lopez is her own woman again. "She has the right stuff on all levels," said *Selena* director Gregory Nava. "She's so focused and talented that she's forced people to accept her for who she is." Whether it's Jennifer, Jenny...

# Jessica Simpson & Nick Lachey

We knew them separately: Jessica Simpson was a pop princess (and avowed virgin) and Nick Lachey was one-fourth of the heartthrob boy band 98°. Together, though, as the stars of MTV's romance reality show *Newlyweds: Nick and Jessica,* they emerged as the It couple of the moment. A very recognizable one too. The fights! The pouting! The tantrums! The cuddling! Cameras in the pair's L.A.-area home caught it all as Simpson proved herself TV's most lovable dumb blonde, unable to do laundry, say platypus or distinguish between chicken and fish. "I know I'm a ditz," she explained breezily. "I'm myself. I can stick my foot in my mouth. I can trip and fall." The ever patient, sports-loving Lachey (the neatnik of the two) invariably picked her up—along with her many shoes—and made his delicate Texas belle go camping (though not without her Louis Vuitton purse). "The thing I learned about Jessica is that she's used to having everything done for her," Lachey said stoically. "I'm a baby," his 23-year-old bride admitted, but that didn't stop the grown-ups at ABC from offering her a sitcom of her own. And to Lachey's relief, Simpson had made progress of another sort: "I hang up my own wet towels now!"

# Tiger Woods

With every helpless golf ball he crushed into the ether, Eldrick "Tiger" Woods blasted his sport to dizzying new heights. "He's playing a game I'm not familiar with," said links legend Jack Nicklaus. With 53 tournament wins, Woods is the leader among active players, the first golfer to simultaneously hold all four major titles and the career money leader—and that doesn't count endorsement deals with American Express and Nike. Though he may live in a glittery cocoon of private jets, chauffeured limos and beautiful women (he's engaged to Swedish au pair Elin Nordegren), Woods has remained his loosey-goosey, video-game-loving self, say friends. Except, of course, when there's a birdie putt on the line. "People talk about Tiger's will to win," said CBS's Peter Kostis, "but I believe his hatred of losing is second to none." Part Thai, Dutch, African-American, Native American and Chinese, he has said, "I don't just want to be the best black player or the best Asian player. I want to be the best golfer ever."

# Halle Berry

Onstage, clutching her Oscar and speaking through her sobs, Halle Berry made a point. "This moment is so much bigger than me," said the first black woman to be named Best Actress (for her role as a downtrodden waitress in 2001's *Monster's Ball*). It was a landmark for Hollywood—and a definite turning point for the former model and Miss U.S.A. runner-up whose previous biggest successes had been in action films like *X-Men* and *Swordfish*. She would soon return to that genre— but this time breaking down another barrier as the first Bond Girl (Jinx) to get equal billing with Pierce Brosnan's 007 in *Die Another Day*. "She has a good sense of her sensuality as a woman," said Brosnan of Berry, who split in 2003 from her second husband, singer Eric Benét. "Plus, she's a very, very good actress." She has risen, said *Die Another Day* director Lee Tamahori, to "that exalted level of American female actors who can command anything she wants."

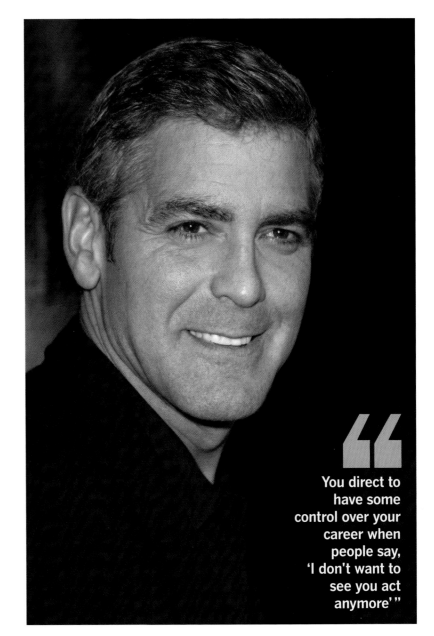

> You direct to have some control over your career when people say, 'I don't want to see you act anymore'"

# George Clooney

We've heard all about his pot-bellied pig and the gang of guys crashing at his L.A. bachelor pad. We've marveled at the gags, the girls, the way he really, really knows how to wear a suit. And yet we've also wondered, exactly what is it about George Clooney that is still so captivating a decade after he first donned scrubs for *ER*? Beyond the matinee-idol mug and fabled charm, "George is a better actor than he thinks he is," said Steven Soderbergh, his director in four films, including *Ocean's Eleven*. Clooney himself made a promising directing debut with 2002's *Confessions of a Dangerous Mind*. He is, by all reports, a generous gent—whether hosting at his 25-room Italian villa or stumping for his congressional candidate dad Nick in Kentucky. Observed the elder Clooney: "He takes care of people."

# Drew
## Barrymore

Sixteen years after she waved goodbye to E.T. as a 6-year-old, Drew Barrymore was still sprinkling her free-spirited pixie dust through *The Wedding Singer.* "The nice thing about Drew," said director Joel Schumacher, "is that she's gotten strong but not tough." He was referring to her dealing with a teenage addiction problem and her famously dysfunctional Hollywood family. In 2000 she moved up to mogul, producing as well as starring in *Charlie's Angels.* So much for the old flake image. "When her business side comes out, it is sharp, succinct and very confident," said Nancy Juvonen, her Flower Films partner. Divorced from her second husband, comedian Tom Green, Barrymore has hung in with refreshing resilience and modesty. "If I ever start talking about 'my craft,' 'my instrument,'" she told one interviewer, "you have permission to shoot me."

# Ellen DeGeneres

She was dubbed the "funniest person in America" by Showtime, hosted both the Grammys and the Emmys, and was a favorite invitee on Leno and Letterman. But when she came out in 1997, on her Top 10 sitcom *Ellen* and in real life, comedian Ellen DeGeneres became both a target and a reluctant gay hero. Backlash from conservatives (Jerry Falwell dubbed her "Ellen DeGenerate") caused some sponsors to bail and ratings to drop. When ABC pulled the plug, DeGeneres said, "I was fired basically because I'm gay." Then, after a very public 2000 breakup, her lover Anne Heche soon began dating now-husband Coleman Laffoon. "Ellen had a lot of healing to do," said actress Kathy Najimy, a close friend. "All the world was watching. She came out, and she went down." Not for long. In 2003 DeGeneres pulled off a heartening bounce back. She was part of the year's top-grossing movie, *Finding Nemo,* as the voice of Dory. And she made her daytime debut with the season's highest-rated new TV talk show—and 12 Emmy nominations. "It's the best job in the world," she said. "I will probably do this for the rest of my career."

# Johnny Depp

When he showed up with gold caps on his teeth to swashbuckle in Disney's *Pirates of the Caribbean* "they thought it was a little much," Johnny Depp recalled of wary film execs. Fortunately, Hollywood's leading eccentric prevailed. The caps (some of them, anyway) stayed for the movie. And his compellingly oddball performance as Captain Jack Sparrow catapulted an art-house fave into Cineplex gold. "I've been very, very lucky," he reflected. "It's amazing I'm still around." Pegged as a rebel on TV's *21 Jump Street,* he hid his chiseled good looks behind bizarre roles in films like *Edward Scissorhands* and *What's Eating Gilbert Grape.* Offscreen he dabbled in drugs, trashed a hotel room and, basically, he admitted, "wasted a whole bunch of time." The turning point? Falling hard for French actress and singer Vanessa Paradis, his lady since 1998. The birth of their two children, he said, "gave me everything. A reason to live. A reason to not be a dumbass. A reason to learn, a reason to breathe, a reason to care."

"Having a child
changes you.
Before him,
I would have
sacrificed myself
completely
for my work"

# Sarah Jessica Parker

She knew what she had to do. After six seductive, saucy and oh-so-satisfying seasons on HBO's *Sex and the City*, it was time for Sarah Jessica Parker to kick off her Manolos and take a well-deserved break. Still, the show's lead actress and executive producer had a hard time leaving her defining role. "Saying goodbye to the cast and crew was like being taken off life support," she said. A showbiz vet who starred on Broadway in *Annie* at 12, Parker was delightful to watch transforming from *Square Pegs* geek to a ditzy babe in *L.A. Story*. Yet it was playing friend extraordinaire and ne'er-do-well-in-love Carrie Bradshaw that turned her into a red-carpet hot mama. The show left her a remembrance of four Golden Globes, but what really keeps her happily around her Manhattan house is James Wilkie, her son with husband Matthew Broderick, born in 2002. Bragging recently, Parker reported that "one of James Wilkie's first words was 'shoe.'" Then the footwear fan couldn't resist adding, "He says it beautifully!"

**Denzel has an extraordinary inner life, and the camera is more than aware of it"**
—Edward Zwick, director of *Glory* and *Courage Under Fire*

# Denzel Washington

In a decade that saw Gibson, Cruise and Costner dominate the box office, Denzel Washington emerged as the first black actor to give the A-list matinee idols a run for the money. His noble bearing, combined with the mostly upstanding, smart characters he played, has made him a thinking woman's heartthrob. After taking on such giants as Malcolm X and South African activist Steven Biko early in his career, Washington explored more tarnished characters like the corrupt cop in *Training Day*, for which he won his second Oscar (his first came for 1989's *Glory*). "He's an architect," said Jonathan Demme, his *Philadelphia* director. "It's just sensational watching him do his thing." In 2002 Washington added a new credit to his résumé with *Antwone Fisher*. Said the father of four: "Directing was such an exhilarating experience. It was the most exciting, fulfilling, stupid, scary thing I ever did."

113

# Julia Roberts

Audiences adore her opposite the nice guy, beaming that smile and tossing that hair through romantic comedies like *My Best Friend's Wedding.* They adore her plucky too, beside stalwart heroes (*The Pelican Brief*) or on her indomitable own as *Erin Brockovich* (her Oscar winner). Small wonder, then, that Julia Roberts was the first actress to earn $20 million a movie. More surprising— and refreshing—was how she poked sly fun at fame itself (*Notting Hill*) and with that big ol' Georgia laugh went on with her life. It has been a full one. After divorcing musician Lyle Lovett, she wed cameraman Danny Moder and added homemaker to her résumé. "There's nothing diva-y at all about Julia," said her *Mona Lisa Smile* costar Marcia Gay Harden. "Our off-set conversations were about whether you should cook the Thanksgiving turkey upside down."

# Will Smith

By many accounts, Will Smith is the most genial man in movies, but he also burns with ambition—and makes no secret of it. He once declared, "I honestly think I could be President of the U.S. if I really wanted to." In the interim, the former rapper and TV star known as the Fresh Prince settled for becoming an action hero, but not the strong, silent sort. In *Independence Day* and his *Men in Black* duo, Smith's do-gooders were gabbers, as quick with wit as with weaponry. "I've created this Will Smith thing that people want to see me do," he noted, before stretching himself—and training for a year—to star in the 2001 bio-drama *Ali* (for which he nabbed an Oscar nod). "He is as successful as he is because people want to be around him. That's so rare," said Smith's *MIB II* costar Lara Flynn Boyle. "Everyone likes Will Smith." In 1997 he wed actress Jada Pinkett, now the mother of two of his three kids. "I'm very comfortable with life in general," he said. "I think that if you put out good energy, you get good energy back."

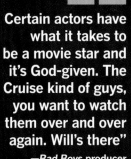

"

Certain actors have what it takes to be a movie star and it's God-given. The Cruise kind of guys, you want to watch them over and over again. Will's there"

—*Bad Boys* producer Jerry Bruckheimer

"

I'm not a
supercool
person. And
I've never
had the
most friends.
I'm a mom
and a wife,
and that's
what I
like to be"

# Reese
## Witherspoon

Before she became a mega-star, Reese Witherspoon once told a reporter that if acting didn't work out she "could be a professional trampolinist." Quite probably the competitive, 5′2″ athlete would have bounced to the top in gymnastics as well. *The New York Times* dubbed her "the most determined actress of the 21st century." The deb daughter of a Nashville surgeon made her debut on the big screen at 14 in the coming-of-age drama *The Man in the Moon* and soon had enough encouraging credits that she could give up on Stanford (and that trampolining fall-back). Triumphs in *Pleasantville, Election* and *Legally Blonde* led to a $15 million take for the sequel *Legally Blonde 2: Red, White and Blonde.* Her fizzy onscreen persona aside, Witherspoon is known as a solid mother to her two young children, Ava and Deacon, with husband Ryan Phillippe. Said Marshall Herskovitz, who directed her in *Jack the Bear*: "She has a great dignity about her that you don't see in people as young as she is." Witherspoon doesn't turn 30 until 2006.

# Prince William

He stands to inherit $1.45 billion, a dozen palaces and (after Charles) the British crown. But as a student at Scotland's University of St. Andrews, the future king has struggled to fit in quietly as William Wales, geography major and ball-cap-wearing regular bloke. "He stands in the queue for his groceries like everybody else," said a St. Andrews local. "There are no superstar tantrums." Recently the 6′3″ heartthrob has been photographed getting cozy with housemate Kate Middleton, outing a relationship the pair had kept secret for a year. While mum on the romance, William has set the record straight on monarchic matters. "Those stories about me not wanting to be king are all wrong," he said in a 21st-birthday interview in '03. "It's a very important role and it's one that I don't take lightly. It's all about helping people and dedication and loyalty, which I hope I have—I know I have."

# Renée Zellweger

She had us at "Hello." But before she wowed audiences as the down-to-earth single mom who heard Tom Cruise whisper "You complete me" in *Jerry Maguire,* Renée Zellweger was continually offered less winning parts. "The other woman, the harlot, the one-night stand," she recalled. "It's a really difficult path to get off." But Zellweger managed, thank you, veering all over the map, playing the neurotic Brit in *Bridget Jones's Diary, Chicago* murderess Roxie Hart and then plain-talkin' country girl Ruby in *Cold Mountain.* Amazingly, all three got her Oscar nominations, and the third, Ruby, was the charm. Defying expectations has come easy for Zellweger, who not only earned De Niro-like props when she bulked up for *Bridget* but won over early naysayers. Her *Nurse Betty* costar Greg Kinnear called her "a really brave actress—she takes roles that scare her a bit." Zellweger wouldn't have it any other way. "I can't make choices based on what other people might think," she said. "I'm acting for myself—for the joy that it brings."

# David Letterman

A lesser man would have been bitter. (Okay, maybe he was a little bitter.) But when he lost Johnny Carson's coveted *Tonight Show* seat to Jay Leno, he bounced back with a bang, defecting from NBC to CBS with his retitled *Late Show with David Letterman*. Armed with his bag of Stupid Pet (and Human) Tricks and the ever-popular Top 10 List, he crafted a quirky and very different kind of talk show. He could be caustic or self-deprecating, with labels like "gap-toothed monkey boy." "I can't sing, dance or act," he once said of hosting. "What else could I be?" But in 2000 it was a kinder, gentler Dave who returned from a hiatus for quintuple-bypass surgery, choking up as he thanked his medical team. He also was an unexpected source of solace to America a week after the 9/11 attacks. "It was Dave's finest hour," said Dan Rather, a guest that first night back. In 2003 longtime girlfriend Regina Lasko gave birth to their son Harry—and a solution to his succession issue. "I can't do this forever," said Letterman, "and it'd be nice to have the kid take over the family business."

**"I'm not going to be around as long as Carson was around. I will leave and go on. You can hear America breathing a sigh of relief"**

**Survivor** If the video-vérité craze germinated with *The Real World,* it turned positively pestilential with the summer 2000 smash *Survivor.* Sixteen strangers were embedded with each other and random actual rodents and insects until all but one was eliminated from their desolate island. **Richard Hatch,** a corporate trainer with a penchant for nudity, out-schemed amiable river guide **Kelly Wiglesworth** for the first $1 million prize. The Darwinian drama proved so popular that the year *Survivor II* was announced, it drew about five times as many applications as the Peace Corps.

# 1995-2004

Scriptwriters, you're fired! The networks—and Nielsen families—opted for a dose of someone else's reality

# REAL

## The Real World

What happens when you throw seven strangers in a house and shoot their unscripted career moves, capers and couplings? The tape would roll 24/7 except, assured the 1992 co-creator Jonathan Murray, "when you're about to score or in the bathroom." Over the years, MTV's *Real World* unveiled roomies both affecting (such as, Pedro Zamora, an AIDS activist from '94 who died of the disease) and absurd (exhibitionists, abusive alcoholics). The 2004 cast (left) bunked in San Diego.

## The Bachelorette

*The Bachelor* debuted in '02, but after five editions, no bachelor has yet tied the knot. Contestant **Trista Rehn** who starred in this '03 spinoff, picked firefighter **Ryan Sutter** from 25 gorgeous guys, and the two of them became the only couple in either series to marry. "We're still going to be in love," she said to cynics' claim that they wed for the $1 mil prize.

## The Apprentice

It was *Survivor* moved to the most treacherous island, Manhattan, with the 16 manipulators being adjudged by the master, Donald Trump. As arch witches like Omarosa got axed, cigar entrepreneur **Bill Rancic** prevailed, ending the three-month ordeal with a $250G gig in the Trump empire.

# WORLD

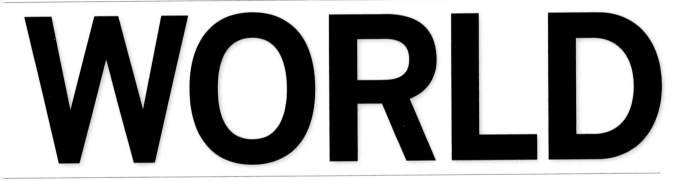

## American Idol

With brutal barbs like "rubbish," or "pathetic," acerbic Brit judge Simon Cowell crushed the dreams of thousands of pop-star wannabes. The few who made it past Cowell and his gentler co-judges, Paula Abdul and Randy Jackson, competed in weekly singathons for the vote and mercy of the viewer masses. Baby-faced Texan **Kelly Clarkson** handily became the Idol in the '02 maiden season. The next year was a saw-off between the so-called Sumo of Soul, **Ruben Studdard,** and **Clay Aiken,** who went from geek to chic during the show. When Studdard won, Claymates (fanatic Aiken rooters) barraged the network, charging a rigged ballot. The rage was not shared by the finalists, who amiably barnstormed the nation on a 39-city *American Idol* mop-up tour.

1995-2004
FIRST-NAME

## Mary-Kate & Ashley

**Last name:** Olsen **Early acclaim:** We've known the twins so long they're practically family. Debuting at 9 months on the ABC sitcom *Full House*—they shared the Michelle Tanner role for eight years—Mary-Kate (left) and Ashley have acted nearly all their lives. **Lil' goldmines:** They've also generated nearly a billion dollars in revenue through videos, movies, books and marketing of their own Wal-Mart clothing and makeup lines. All this *before* college—they are due to enter New York University in fall '04. Conceded Robert Thorne, CEO of the twins' entertainment conglomerate Dualstar: Mary-Kate and Ashley "are a property now, aside from being people with a heartbeat."

# BASIS

Was it their body of work (Shania, Leo) or the oddity of their monikers (Calista, Charlize) that made them one-name wonders? And will we always have Paris?

# Gwyneth

**Last name:** Paltrow **Great expectations:** The brainy daughter of actress Blythe Danner and TV producer Bruce Paltrow went for and got a major film role, Wendy in Steven Spielberg's *Hook,* at 18, despite Mom's hopes that she'd be "the next Margaret Mead." **Critics' darling:** Won raves for *Emma,* then nabbed a Best Actress Oscar for *Shakespeare in Love* at 26. She tearfully accepted in a pink Ralph Lauren gown that cemented her fashion icon status. **Leading men:** With a succession of old flames that included Brad Pitt, Ben Affleck and Luke Wilson, she was ranked by paparazzi as one of their top five subjects. Then in 2003, the part-time Londoner announced her pregnancy and surprise marriage to Coldplay frontman Chris Martin.

# Calista

**Last name:** Flockhart **Case history:** After a few stage roles and the film *The Birdcage,* Flockhart broke out in FOX's *Ally McBeal.* The neurotic young lawyer pined for her ex who worked at the same firm, shared the bathroom with male coworkers and wore the skimpiest of skirts to court. **Nest mates:** At 36 she adopted son Liam, who joins Mom on outings with her beau of two years, Harrison Ford.

# Leonardo

**Last name:** DiCaprio **Dry run:** A stint on ABC's *Growing Pains* was followed by film stardom in the edgy *Romeo + Juliet.* But it was by playing another doomed lover, Jack Dawson in 1997's *Titanic,* that DiCaprio bobbed to heartthrob status at 23. Only five weeks after the opening, Fox estimated that 7 percent of all U.S. teenage girls had seen it at least twice. Said one breathless fan: "His existence has forever changed my life." **Calmer waters:** The following year DiCaprio took time off, kicking back and partying with pals, including supermodel Gisele Bündchen, his off-and-now-on-again lady. By '02 he returned in the epic *Gangs of New York.* "I guess I just never want to be in that 'whatever happened? You used to love me' situation," he said.

# Celine

**Last name:** Dion *Quelle histoire!* Since releasing her first U.S. CD in 1990, the French-Canadian singer has given birth to son René-Charles, helped husband René Angélil beat neck cancer and won five Grammys, including two for her career-making *Titanic* hit, "My Heart Will Go On." **The jackpot:** She is currently in the second year of a Las Vegas extravaganza scheduled to run all the way into 2006. In addition to her $100 million contract, the temporary relocation to Vegas, she said, would "provide stability for my family" and "freedom onstage." Cost of the 4,148-seat Colosseum, constructed just for her at Caesars Palace? $95 million. Top price for a ticket? A record $225.

# P. Diddy

**Real name:** Sean Combs **Rap start:** He made his earlier name—Puff Daddy—as the 20ish hip-hop impresario who launched Mary J. Blige and the Notorious B.I.G. Next he took on fashion, introducing his own clothing line, Sean John, in 1998. **Remix:** After being charged with gun possession in 1999—he was later acquitted—he split from then girlfriend Jennifer Lopez and rechristened himself P. Diddy. ("Most people call me Diddy," he says.) Newly buff, he ran the 2003 New York City Marathon to raise money for charity.

# Eminem

**Real name:** Marshall Mathers III **Incendiary arrival:** A ninth-grade dropout, the pasty poet-rapper debuted in '99 with *The Slim Shady LP.* His second CD, equally polarizing (homophobic, misogynist—and, raved critics, brilliant), won two Grammys; he has seven in all. In 2002 he was cheered for his acting in the roughly autobiographical *8 Mile.* **Family values:** The self-described "Mr. Potty-Mouth King" permitted his 8-year-old daughter to hear only sanitized versions of his songs.

# Angelina

**Last name:** Jolie (she dropped dad Jon Voight's last name after following him into acting) **Kudos:** She received a Best Supporting Actress Oscar as a sociopath for 1999's *Girl, Interrupted.* **Dark side:** She is long estranged from her father, who said she "has found very clever ways to mask her extreme problems." She wore a necklace containing a drop of then husband Billy Bob Thornton's blood. **Turnabout:** After adopting son Maddox in Cambodia, the *Tomb Raider* star and Thornton split. She became a U.N. activist and devoted single mom. "For me," she said, "becoming a parent changed everything."

## Paris

**Last name:** Hilton **Precocious youth:** Raised in Manhattan and L.A., the 1981-born hotel-chain heiress upstaged sister Nicky to become her generation's pre-eminent party girl. And that was *before* a sex tape with an ex-boyfriend created an Internet sensation. **Sex and the country:** She and pal Nicole Richie be-guiled Arkansas farm boys on FOX's reality series *The Simple Life*—a smash that led to guest gigs on *The O.C.* and *Las Vegas*.

## Shania

**Real name:** Eilleen Edwards (Twain came from her Ojibway stepdad; Shania means "I'm on my way") **Heroic beginnings:** Family often went without electricity in rural Canadian home. At 22 she put her career on hold to raise three younger siblings after their parents died in a car crash. **Reversal of fortune:** Her 1997 *Come on Over* became the best-selling album ever by a female artist. **Still the one:** She shared three (of her five) Grammys with producer husband "Mutt" Lange. After taking a three-year break with their son in Switzerland, she came roaring back with 2002's *Up!*

## Matt & Katie

**Last names:** Lauer & Couric **Ratings impact:** Nielsens soared when he replaced Bryant Gumbel as her cohost on NBC's *Today* in 1997. **Mr. Hunk/Ms. Spunk:** She has likened their chemistry to "two kids in high school who are buddies but a little competitive." **Compensation for lousy hours:** A four-and-a-half-year $65 million contract for her; a three-year $8 million extension for him.

# Ben

**Last name:** Affleck **Extreme visibility:**
After winning a Best Screenplay Oscar
for 1997's *Good Will Hunting,* which
he and Matt Damon costarred in and
wrote, Affleck became a leading man
in *Pearl Harbor.* He also took up with
two very famous women—Gwyneth
Paltrow and then Jennifer Lopez—
and was dogged by the paparazzi whom
such luminous couplings attract. The
latter pairing—soon known the world
over as Bennifer—filmed the turkey
*Gigli* before splitting in early 2004. **Rep
rehab:** Having completed an alcohol-
abuse program in '01, Affleck can
weather trouble. Assured director pal
Kevin Smith: "He's the same old Ben."

# Charlize

**Last name:** Theron **Foreign study:** At 19, the willowy South African farm girl moved to L.A. to act. She lost her accent watching Nickelodeon and *Love Boat* reruns and won a part in 1996's *That Thing You Do!* **Monstrous triumph:** After years of playing gorgeous girlfriends, she transformed herself into unlovely serial killer Aileen Wuornos to play the lead in 2003's *Monster.* The payoff for her 30-lb. weight gain and denuded eyebrows? Critical kudos—"one of the greatest performances in the history of cinema," raved Roger Ebert—and an Oscar.

# Justin

**Last name:** Timberlake **Résumé:** A former Mousketeer who stole hearts as the breakout star of teen phenom 'N Sync, he stayed true for four years to girlfriend Britney Spears. **His way:** By 2002 he had split with Spears and released a solo CD, *Justified,* that went multiplatinum. **Superstorm:** Performing before a TV audience of zillions at the 2004 Super Bowl, he ripped the bodice of Janet Jackson, exposing her breast. The incident, he explained coyly, was "a wardrobe malfunction."

# Christina

**Last name:** Aguilera **Upward mobility:** She needed only three years to turn herself from perky popster (1999's "Genie in a Bottle") to brazen "Dirrty" girl. More recently she shot an ad campaign for Versace while glamming up her own image. She also toured with a fellow Mickey Mouse Club alum, Justin Timberlake (above, right), kissed Madonna during an awards show (who hasn't?) and changed her hair color twice within a year. **New attitude:** She began dissing other singers, claiming they "aren't artists, they're just performers—fake and superficial."

# Ashton

**Last name:** Kutcher (he's really Christopher Ashton Kutcher) **Serious crush:** Playing doofy hunk Kelso on FOX's *That '70s Show,* and later as the mischief-making host of MTV's *Punk'd,* he bowled over teenage audiences. **Family guy:** Next, at 25, he famously bowled over Demi Moore—then 40—not to mention her ex Bruce Willis and their three daughters. Kutcher and Moore were even parrying rumors of a summer 2004 wedding. But despite all the sudden buzz, observed *'70s Show* costar Mila Kunis, "he's still the same little Iowa boy."

# FALLS FROM GRACE

Divorce and impeachment and show trials: Oh, my! When celebrities tumble from their pedestals, the thuds can resound round the world

## Bill Clinton & Monica Lewinsky

### A tryst nearly deposed a President

As White House scandals go, Monicagate was one of the more tawdry. Facing charges of sexual harassment from Paula Jones, a semen-stained blue dress and Monica Lewinsky's conversations about her affair with him (taped by her former friend Linda Tripp), Bill Clinton became only the second President to be impeached. For months he had denied the relationship with the 23-year-old intern, and his wife, Hillary, had blamed the accusations on a "vast right-wing conspiracy." Eventually acquitted by the Senate in 1999, he is now on the lecture circuit and acts as unofficial consultant to the Democratic senator from New York, Hillary Rodham Clinton. Lewinsky has dabbled in handbag design, among other careers. "I'm not going to pretend that it was always about something bigger than me," Lewinsky said of the scandal. "Because for me, it wasn't."

# Rosie O'Donnell

## In a court battle, daytime TV's Queen of Nice tarnished her crown

Fans who watched her adoring—often fawning—schmoozefests on *The Rosie O'Donnell Show* got a not-so cutie patootie glimpse of the host's darker side when she went to court against magazine publisher Gruner + Jahr. In 2002, six months after she came out of the closet on national TV and four months after she ended her Emmy-winning talk show to spend more time with her family, O'Donnell abruptly shut down her namesake magazine, *Rosie,* following an acrimonious feud with G + J about its editorial direction. The publishing giant fired back, filing a lawsuit accusing the comic of "bizarre and oft-times mean-spirited behavior" (a former staffer—a breast-cancer survivor—testified that O'Donnell had told her that "liars get cancer"). G + J sought damages in excess of $100 million; O'Donnell countersued for $125 million. But the judge declared the case a draw after a seven-week trial. "I have never wanted anything but peace," said O'Donnell. The mother of four then waded into another controversy—the gay-marriage debate—marrying longtime partner Kelli Carpenter in San Francisco.

11/20
Photo
NAM
RAC:
DOB:
HGT:
BLD:
HAI:
MKS:
BOO

## Liza Minnelli & David Gest
### A match made in showbiz ended in a divorce from hell

The ludicrously overplanned 2002 wedding of Liza Minnelli and David Gest brought out what one witness called "the biggest freak show in the world"—1,000 close friends, including Liz Taylor, Michael Jackson and Mickey Rooney. The marriage itself—all 16 months of it—brought out the worst in both. After they split in 2003, they each filed for divorce, with Gest citing repeated beatings by Minnelli. He claimed he also experienced vertigo, nausea, hypertension, mood swings, insomnia, "scalp tenderness" and "unrelenting pain in his head." Minnelli's $2 million countersuit claimed that Gest messed up as her agent, "refusing projects unless they included himself" and that he "constantly berated Minnelli in public and began holding himself out as the 'star.'" No word on whether the wedding gifts were returned.

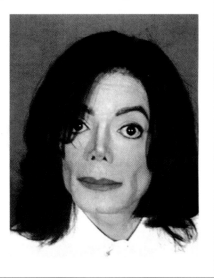

nta Barbara County Sheriff's Dept.

SON, MICHAEL
SEX: M
58 AGE: 45
WGT: 120
CMP:
EYE: BRO

621785

## Michael Jackson
### A superstar faced unsettling charges and an uncertain future

It wasn't the first time Michael Jackson had to answer such disturbing allegations. But after a 2003 arrest warrant accusing him of sexually molesting a 13-year-old boy and giving him an "intoxicating agent," the singer had to surrender to police and wound up handcuffed and depicted in a surreal mug shot. Months earlier, in a British TV documentary about him, Jackson said that he had slept with "many children" at his Neverland ranch and described the practice as "the most loving thing." Then, in April 2004, a California grand jury issued a 10-count indictment charging him with child molestation and conspiracy to abduct a child. (The boy's parents alleged that Jackson aides tried to persuade the family to leave the country.) Jackson, who could face 20 years in prison, pleaded not guilty to all counts.

## Winona Ryder

### Caught in the act, a troubled actress paid her debt

Despite being able to haul in some $5 million a film, two-time Oscar nominee Winona Ryder was accused of walking into the Beverly Hills Saks Fifth Avenue and trying to make off with $5,560.40 in merchandise, including a Gucci dress, a Marc Jacobs top, a Dolce & Gabbana bag, a rhinestone hair band and seven pairs of designer socks. Although in the months after her arrest she kept a Gen-Xer's curled upper lip—doing the hip-ironic thing by appearing on a *W* cover in a "Free Winona" T-shirt—she had effectively discounted herself into that bargain basement of baffling dysfunctional stars. Not taking the stand in her seven-day trial, Ryder made her statement through fashion, arriving for court in a parade of demure outfits. Her attorney argued that a woman of such taste would never steal that headband. The jury didn't buy it. Found guilty, she was sentenced to three years' probation, $10,000 in fines and 480 hours of community service. Reality bites, indeed.

## Martha Stewart

### A domestic diva faces the big house

For Martha Stewart, having friends in high places turned out to be not such a good thing. Her sale of 4,000 shares of ImClone stock led to accusations that she had received an insider tip. She was charged with making false statements, obstruction of justice and securities fraud. (The heads-up came from her broker's assistant rather than her pal Dr. Sam Waksal, the pharmaceutical company's founder and CEO.) VIP supporters called it a bitch hunt. "There are a lot of people who don't wish her well," said ad man Jerry Della Femina. The six-week trial was a media circus and fuel for late-night funsters. Found guilty on four felony charges, Stewart planned an appeal and resigned from the board of her multimillion-dollar firm, Martha Stewart Living Omnimedia, remaining as "founding editorial director." "I feel sad," she said, "but I'm not guilty."

# Janet Jackson & Justin Timberlake
## Two pop stars stole the Super Bowl

Halftime shows have come a long way from twirlers and marching bands. After Justin Timberlake tore away part of Janet Jackson's costume at the 2004 Super Bowl, revealing a sunburst nipple shield, TiVos across America went into overdrive and the Federal Communications Commission quickly called it a "classless, crass and deplorable stunt." CBS made on-air apologies a condition for the performers to appear on the Grammys. Timberlake said okay, Jackson didn't. The peekaboo show's fallout? An FCC probe and hypervigilant TV censors.

**Plasma Screens** When unveiled in 1998, they cost a prohibitive $15,000. Now down to about $3,000, these pleasingly thin sets (their flat panels are filled with pixels of gas that allow for a high-definition picture) and the LCD versions command some 5 percent of the TV market.

**Logo Mania** What's in a name? Carried by the likes of Madonna, Eve and Jessica Simpson, the Murakami earned Louis Vuitton more than $300 million in 2003. Meanwhile, the Burberry pattern was splashed on everyone from your neighbor to her Scottish terrier, Dior stamped its label on its ostentatious saddle bags, and Chanel ventured to lend its chic to a snowboard.

# Manolo Blahniks

With a huge plug from Carrie's endless obsession on *Sex and the City,* this luscious brand became a household name. The $400-plus beauties have become a must-have in every aspiring fashionista's wardrobe.

**Low-Rise Jeans** Just when you thought they couldn't go lower, **Christina Aguilera** et al were baring more and more of their enviable bellies, earning beaucoup bucks for Earl Jean, Seven for All Mankind and Paper Denim & Cloth.

## Pokémon

A wave of invaders with funny names—Pikachu, Snorlax and Charizard—established a U.S. beachhead in 1998 and captured the 4- to 12-year-old crowd. The Pokémon tsunami had hit first in Japan two years earlier. Eventually amassing more than $6 billion in sales for Nintendo ($1 billion in the U.S.) from movies, TV shows, video games and trading cards, these "pocket monsters" seemed to bewildered parents more like pocket pickers.

### Chandelier Earrings

They're painfully weighty on the lobes, but these oversize ornaments, which hit big in 2003, were so fun and flattering, aficionados like Sandra Bullock began sporting them at events less elegant than the Oscars. Now a favorite look for daytime, the jeweled danglers add star power even to casual outfits.

### Red Bull

What's *in* this stuff?! Such is the frequently asked question of those who find the energy drink quite invigorating indeed. One key ingredient? Taurine, an amino acid already present in the human body. Mixed with vodka, the Austrian beverage has been a fizzy hit on the U.S. bar circuit since 2000.

### Apple iPod

Released just in time for Christmas 2001, the easy-to-use iPod made MP3s the norm in listening. While other brands have come up with copycat versions, Apple's ever-evolving sleek design is what's keeping the cooler kids—and adults—in tune.

iPod
Playlists >
Browse >
Extras >
Settings >
Backlight

# FADS & FASHIONS
## 1995-2004

Low-rise jeans and Manolos may have legs, but pashminas or Pokémon? Nope

## Boy Bands

When the Backstreet Boys arrived in '97, teen girls couldn't get enough. More hit acts soon followed, like 'N Sync and 98°, but solo careers grew too tempting for the boys to band together forever.

## Thongs

Put it away, ladies! The point of a thong was to avoid panty lines, so why did so many show them off? The skimpy skivvies remain practical, but no one need know they're there.

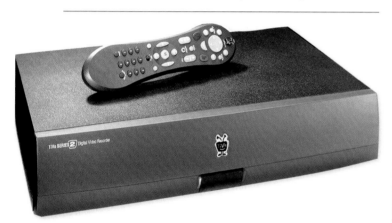

## TiVo

Aimed at rendering VCRs obsolete, the digital video recording device signed on a million homes since '99. You can pause live TV when Aunt Rose calls, skip past commercials or ogle Janet Jackson in slo-mo. Most turn off the feature that records programs TiVo *thinks* you'd like, though. *Yes, Dear?* Oh no.

## Scooters

Walking became a passé mode of transportation the summer of 2000, when everyone from schoolkids to spirited suits hopped on their Razor scooters to zip to their destination in a speedy, eco-friendly style. Weighing just six pounds and collapsing to make for easy carriage, the $119 scooter became the Sharper Image's top seller. By the next year most reverted to more old-fashioned forms of travel.

## Botox

This toxin, which temporarily paralyzes one's muscles, has won over millions of devotees, including admitted user Melissa Rivers. Though the shots make it more difficult to express oneself, that's the price for being as wrinkle-free as a polyester jacket.

## Trucker Hats

Faking the blue-collar, man-of-the-people look with a designer version was a fun idea, popularized in part by Ashton Kutcher. But at $50 plus, the mesh caps are a laugh that may not last.

# Juicy Couture suits

Comfy and cute, these sweat sets (running around $200 each) are a fave among celebrities and style-conscious civilians alike. Some more daring fans even sported a version that spelled out "juicy" across the backside.

## Pashminas

Made from super-soft cashmere from Himalayan goats, these pricey shawls heated up fast. Luminaries like Liv Tyler would sooner have stayed home than hit the red carpet without one. But that was '00, and with the masses buying cut-rate silk "fauxminas," the trend soon became overexposed—and then a wrap.

## Ugg Boots

Born in Australia as a means of keeping surfers warm, these sheepskins got a foothold in California in 2003 and stomped east. Worn with everything from jeans to miniskirts, they were soon back-ordered and inevitably copied by the boot-company competition.

## Starbucks

From its first Seattle store in '71, this coffee chain boomed in the '90s with rich roasts and a complex ordering system. Vente half-caf low-fat caramel macchiato, anyone?

## Hair Extensions

Anyone wishing for more Rapunzelian locks, like heiress Paris Hilton, no longer had to endure years of growing her hair out before seeing results. Either sewn in or glued strand by strand by a hairdresser, or simply attached with a clip, the extensions trend began in '98 and grew to great lengths.

# INDEX

# PICTURE CREDITS

**MASTHEAD/CONTENTS**
**2-3** (clockwise from left)
Bruce McBroom/MPTV;
David Levenson/Rex USA;
Lisa O'Connor/Zuma

**ICONS 1974-1984**
**4-5** Gilbert Uzan/Gamma
**6** Bruce McBroom/MPTV
**7** Michael Childers/Corbis
Sygma **8-9** Baron Wolman/
Retna **10** E.J. Camp/Corbis
Outline **11** (from top) Theo
Westenberger; Screenscenes
**12** Hulton-Deutsch Collection/
Corbis **13** Douglas Kirkland/
Corbis **14-15** Gunther/MPTV
**16** (from top) John Springer
Collection/Corbis; Greg
Gorman/Corbis Outline
**17** Douglas Kirkland/Corbis
**18** Douglas Kirkland/Corbis
**19** Time-Life/Getty **20-21**
Hulton-Deutsch Collection/
Corbis **22** Jorie Gracen/
London Features **23** Douglas
Kirkland/Corbis **24-25**
Douglas Kirkland/Corbis
Sygma; Neil Leifer **26-27** Lynn
Goldsmith/Corbis (2)

**SEXY SOAPS**
**28-29** (clockwise from left)
ABC Photo Archives; Globe;
Photofest; Phil Roach/Ipol;
CBS Photo Archive (2)

**STRONG WOMEN
SENSITIVE MEN**
**30-31** (from left) Corbis/
Bettmann; Shepard Sherbell/
Corbis Saba; Globe; Corbis
Bettmann **32-33** (clockwise
from top left) Photofest;
Corbis Bettmann (2); Photo-
fest; Corbis Bettmann (2)

**ROCKIN' ROLES**
**34** Globe **35** MPTV **36-37**
(clockwise from left) Photofest; Universal/Shooting Star;
Yoram Kahana/Shooting Star;
MPTV; Steven Tackeff/Zuma;
**38-39** (clockwise from left)
CBS Photo Archive; Lynn
Goldsmith/Corbis; M. Paris-
ian/Shooting Star; MPTV;
©Henson Associates; Photofest

**FADS & FASHIONS 1974-84**
**40-41** (clockwise from left)
Courtesy of Sony Electronics;
Photofest; Stefano Bianchetti/
Corbis; Corbis/Bettmann;
C. Thomson/Woodfin Camp;
Steve Labadessa (2) **42-43**
(clockwise from top left)
Raeanne Rubenstein; Jacques
Chenet/Time-Life/Getty;
Robin Platzer/Time-Life/
Getty; Globe; Time-Life

Books; Norman Seeff; Steve
Labadessa **44-45** (clockwise
from top left) Al Freni/ Time
Life/Getty; SMP/Globe; Neal
Peters Collection; Hulton
Archive/Getty; MPTV; Neal
Preston/Corbis

**ICONS 1985-1994**
**46-47** Ken Goff/Getty **48-49**
(from left) Sam Emerson/
Polaris; Fabrizio Bensch/
Reuters/Landov; Tobias
Schwartz/Reuters/Landov
**50** Alfred Eisenstadt/Time
Life/Getty **51** Herb Ritts/
Visages **52-53** Dana Fineman
**54-55** (from left) Everett;
Aaron Rapoport; 20th Cen-
tury Fox/Photofest **56-57**
(from left) Peggy Sirota/
Corbis; Greg Gorman/Corbis
**58-59** (from left) Robert
Trachtenberg/Corbis; Herb
Ritts/Visages **60-61** Walter
Iooss Jr./NBAE/Getty
**62** Youri Lenquette/Retna
**63** Andrew Eccles/JBG Photo
**64-65** Dana Fineman
**66-67** (from top left) Jean
Pagliuso/Corbis; Globe; Kim
Komenich/Time-Life/Getty

**MUST-SEE SITCOMS**
**66-67** (clockwise from top
left) NBC/Globe; Carin Baer/
Castle Rock Entertainment;
Viacom/Photofest; CBS/
Landov; NBC/Globe; Para-
mount Pictures/Photofest

**OVER THE TOP!**
**70-71** Adam Scull/Globe
**72-73** (clockwise from top
left) Douglas Kirkland/Corbis
Sygma; Everett; Neal Peters
Collection; Frank Griffin/
London Features; J. Marma-
ras/Woodfin Camp **74-75**
(from left) Joyce Ravid/Corbis;
Everett; Michael Putland/
Retna; Timothy White/Corbis
Outline; Michael Putland/
Retna **76-77** (clockwise from
bottom left) Kevin Winter/
DMI/Getty; All American TV;
DMI/Getty; Everett; Lynn
Goldsmith/Corbis

**SCANDALS**
**78-79** (from left) Reuters/
Landov; Rick Meyer/LA Times/
Abaca **80-81** (clockwise from
top left) Mike Alexander/Cor-
bis Bettmann; Time Life/DMI/
Getty; Pascal Rondeau/All-
sport/Getty; Intersport; Chuck
Burton/AP; Greg Gibson/
Corbis Bettmann **82-83** (from
left) John Loengard; National
Enquirer/Getty **84-85** (from

top left) David Burnett/Con-
tact; Terry Ashe/Getty; Corbis
Sygma; Greta Pratt/Reuters/
Corbis; Terry Ashe/Getty

**FADS & FASHIONS 1985-94**
**86-87** (clockwise from left)
Julio Donaso/Corbis Sygma;
Rocky W. Widner/Retna;
Nintendo Properties used
with permission/courtesy
of Nintendo; Garth Vaughan
**88-89** (clockwise from
bottom left) John Barr/
Liaison/Getty; ©Hasbro,Inc.
2004; Michael Calil/Rex USA;
Frank Ockenfels/Corbis
Outline; Deborah Feingold/
Corbis Outline; Jeff Kravitz/
Filmmagic; Al Freni/Time
Life/Getty **90-91** (clockwise
from left) E.J. Camp/Corbis
Outline; Josh McHugh;
Urbano DelValle; Scott
Weiner/Retna; Fox Children's
Network/Foto Fantasies;
MPTV; Charles Hoselton/
Retna; Globe

**ICONS 1995-2004**
**92-93** James White/Corbis
Outline **94** Rizzo/Sipa
**95** Ruven Afanador/Corbis
Outline **96** Erik C. Pendzich/
Rex USA; **97** Brooks Kraft/
Gamma **98-99** Peggy Sirota/
Corbis Outline **100** Mark
Liddell/Icon **101** Suzuki K
**102-103** (from left) ©2004
Fabrizio Ferri/Harpo Produc-
tions Inc; Roger Karnbad/
Celebrity Photo; Wally Skalij/
Abaca **104** Contour Photos
**105** Jim Wright/Icon **106** Cliff
Watts/Icon **107** Jen Lowery/
London Features **108-109**
Kenneth Willardt **110** Michele
Laurita-Wickman/Corbis
Outline **111** Nigel Parry/CPI
**112** Wayne Maser/Icon **113**
Sante D'Orazio/Corbis Out-
line **114** Sante D'Orazio/Cor-
bis Outline **115** Jean-Francois
Robert/Corbis Outline **116-117**
Mary Ellen Matthews/Corbis
Outline; Tim Graham/Corbis
Sygma **118** Jack Guy/Corbis
Outline **119** © 2004
CBS/Worldwide Pants

**REAL WORLD**
**120-121** (clockwise from
top left) CBS/Landov; Dan
Steinberg/BEImages;
Lawrence Lucier/Filmmagic;
Lucy Nicholson/AP; Lucy
Nicholson/Reuters/Landov;
Scott Allegri/Getty

**FIRST-NAME BASIS**
**122-123** Art Streiber/Icon

**124** DF/London Features
**125** (clockwise from top left)
Steve Sands/New York
Newswire/Corbis Sygma;
Gilbert Flores/Celebrity
Photo; Abaca **126** (from top)
Vanit/Retna; James K. Burns/
Camera Press/Retna **127**
Robert Erdmann/Icon **128**
(clockwise from left) Kevin
Mazur/Wireimage; George
Holtz/JBG Photo; Erin Patrice
O'Brien/Corbis Outline **129**
Herb Ritts/Visages **130** Dan
Kulu/Vanit/Retna **131** (clock-
wise from top left) George
Pimental/Wireimage; Chris
Polk/Filmmagic; Peter Brew-
Bevan/Headpress/Retna

**FALLS FROM GRACE**
**132-133** Corbis Sygma
**134-135** (clockwise from
left) Mark Mainz/Getty;
Sang Tan/AP; Reuters/
Landov **136-137** Rex USA;
Frank Micelotta/Getty;
Reuters/Landov; (2) Bebeto
Matthews/AP

**FADS & FASHIONS
1995-2004**
**138** (clockwise from top left)
David Lazarus; Chris
Weeks/Filmmagic; Urbano
DelValle; Courtesy Louis
Vuitton Multi-Color Speedy
Bag **139** (clockwise from top
left) Fitzroy Barrett/Globe;
Neal Peters Collection; Davies
+ Starr; Anthony Verde/Time-
Life/Getty **140** (clockwise
from top left) Startracks/Rex
USA; Rudy Archuleta/Redux;
Todd Huffman; John Muggen-
borg; Jonathan Friolo/Globe;
Courtesy Tivo **141** (clockwise
from top left) Ned Matura;
Stephen Chernin/Getty;
Henry McGee/Globe; John
Muggenborg; Ronald Sie-
moneit/Corbis Sygma

**COVER**
Kenneth Willardt; **Cover
Insets:** (softcover only) (from
top) Chris Weeks/Filmmagic;
Kathryn Indiek/Globe; Jeffrey
Mayer/Wireimage

**BACK COVER**
(softcover) (from left)
Lionel Hahn/Abaca; Gilbert
Flores/Celebrity Photo;
Tsuni/Gamma; Steve Granitz/
Wireimage; Kevin Winter/
Getty (hardcover) (from left)
Lionel Hahn/Abaca; Kevin
Winter/Getty; Tsuni/Gamma;
Kathryn Indiek/Globe;
Carolyn Contni/Beimages